Southern Railway's Spencer Shops

1896–1996

by
Duane Galloway and Jim Wrinn

1996
TLC Publishing Inc.
Route 4, Box 154
Lynchburg, Va 24503-9711

Front Cover Illustration:
In this painting specially commissioned for this book, Andrew Harmantas shows Southern Railway Mountain-type locomotive No. 1480 riding the turntable in front of the Bob Julian Roundhouse on a fine day in the 1940s. In the rear at left, Spencer Shops' own creation, streamlined No.1380 for *The Tennessean*, waits its turn while an Asheville-bound Santa Fe-type, right, peers from the roundhouse.

Back Cover Illustration: These two postcard views show the Spencer Shops complex in the 1930's when repairing and running steam locomotives was the main reason for this railroad center's existance.

Bottom: The cavernous Spencer Shops back shop in a early 1900's view shows the scores of tools and machines that were needed by the hundreds of men to keep the Southern Railway's steam locomotives going.

Endsheets This wonderful view from 1938 was featured in a *Life* magazine article on the Southern Railway centering around Spencer. *Time-Life*

Library of Congress Catalogue Card Number 96-61074
ISBN 1-883089-23-9

Layout and Design by Kenneth L. Miller
Miller Design & Photography, Salem, Va.

Printed by
Walsworth Publishing Co.
Marceline, Mo. 64658

Table of Contents

Dedication iv

Acknowledgments iv

Introduction v

Chapter 1

Setting the Stage 1

Chapter 2

Building the Shops and Town 7

Chapter 3

Early Growth of the Shops, 1900-1917 15

Chapter 4

The Town of Spencer, 1900-1920 25

Chapter 5

Expansion of Southern Railway, Spencer Shops and the Town of Spencer 31

Chapter 6

The Spencer Worker 41

Chapter 7

Following a Locomotive through Inspection and Repair 53

Chapter 8

Trade Unions and Strikes 61

Chapter 9

The Daily Grind 67

Chapter 10

The Diesel Era 77

Chapter 11

The Demise of the Spencer Shops 89

Chapter 12

Spencer Shops: The Museum 97

Acknowledgments

The authors are deeply indebted to many people for making this work possible. First is Dr. Richard F. Knapp of North Carolina Historic Sites, who kept this work moving forward despite formidable obstacles. The staff of Historic Sites and the staff and volunteers at the North Carolina Transportation Museum (NCTM) provided much assistance.

Several people went beyond the call. Marvin Rogers and Paul Hess made their photo collections available. Rick Jackson printed many vintage views. W. Calvin and Nancy Reynolds were instrumental in the final product. Southern Railway historian Dale Roberts provided superb context. Shirley Napier read the manuscript and made valuable suggestions.

The Southern Railway Historical Association provided photos from its remarkable David Driscoll Collection. The association, founded at Spencer Shops in 1986, publishes a newsletter called *Ties* and actively works to promote Southern Railway history. Readers may contact SRHA at P.O. Box 33, Spencer, N.C. 28159.

Information about the museum is available from NCTM, Box 165, Spencer, N.C. 28159, telephone (704) 636-2889.

Dedication

To the Spencer Shops employees whose monumental labor made the wheels go around a long time ago and to the tireless workers and volunteers of the North Carolina Transportation Museum who remind us of that tremendous effort every day.

North Carolina Division of Archives and History
Employees of the tender shop at Spencer gather for a group portrait in the early 1900s.

Introduction

Talk about unsung heroes.

That's the real story of Spencer Shops — the people working at a big-time railroad repair center but virtually unknown outside the railroad industry. Ballads were written about brave engineers. Books were penned about fast freights and sleek passenger trains. But little thought was given to the army of workers who made it all possible. For every thundering freight train wheeling textiles, tobacco, and furniture out of North Carolina, hundreds labored in the cavernous Spencer back shop. For every one of the 22 daily passenger trains rolling along the Southern Railway main line between Washington and Atlanta, scores of men (and sometimes women) toiled in the smoky, noisy roundhouse or any one of the buildings scattered around the Spencer Shops.

For too long, railway history has focused on the train and the locomotive, paying little attention to one of railroading's most important occupations: its repair and maintenance workers. They put in hundreds of hours of work for each hour a steam engine spent on the main line. Pages of copy and thousands of pictures have shown trains and locomotives in operation. Few were made to document what it took to keep them going. The behind-the-scenes players have gained little notice.

This omission is tragic considering railroading's key contributions to building the New South in the late 1800s and early 1900s. Trains that carried the South's commerce and populace would never have turned a wheel without boilermakers, blacksmiths, and laborers. The communities that sprouted up around repair centers are themselves noteworthy.

The work that once took place at Spencer is far from unique. On the Southern Railway, Spencer was the largest steam repair shop but far from the only one. Similar work took place at Coster Shops in Knoxville, Pegram Shops in Atlanta, and other places. In North Carolina shopmen toiled on engines, freight cars, and passenger cars at numerous locations where roundhouses and repair shops sprang up. They also adjusted main driving rods, filled sand domes, and packed journals for two other important main line railways operating in the state. The Seaboard Air Line employed shopmen at Hamlet in the Sandhills area of North Carolina. Further east, the Atlantic Coast Line's Emerson Shops at Rocky Mount kept up steam locomotives and passenger cars.

Nationally, important railroad shops dotted the landscape on every railroad: Belen, New Mexico, on the Santa Fe; Roseville, California, on the Southern Pacific; Cheyenne, Wyoming, on the Union Pacific; South Louisville on the Louisville & Nashville; Altoona, Pennsylvania, on the Pennsylvania; Colonie, New York, on the Delaware & Hudson; Clifton Forge, Virginia, on the Chesapeake & Ohio; and Roanoke, Virginia, on the Norfolk and Western. The story that unfolded at Spencer took place in countless communities.

For that reason, it is appropriate that Spencer Shops is listed on the National Register of Historic Places and is home to the North Carolina Transportation Museum. So many steam-era railway shops have closed, as Spencer did, only to become forgotten. Bulldozed or converted to other industries, they quickly fade from memory. At Spencer, visitors stand in awe of the size of this complex that dwarfs many modern industrial facilities. In preservation, the Spencer Shops remind us of the American steam locomotive shop — the barn for the iron horse. They speak of the incredible effort needed to keep the engines of American commerce moving. They tell tales of heroes who did their jobs with professionalism and pride, ensuring prompt delivery of goods and safety of crews and passengers. They remind us of an America before the computer, before robotic assembly lines, before automated workplaces, when the story was one of men and machines.

Jim Wrinn
Duane Galloway
Spencer, N.C.
September 1996

Shop switcher No. 1575, an 0-6-0T, is undergoing repair on
September 15, 1946

Setting the Stage:
The Southern Railway and a New Shop Complex

The story of Spencer Shops begins with a tale of financial collapse and renewal.

The Southern Railway Company was formed in 1894, rising Phoenix-like from the ashes of the bankrupt Richmond & Danville Railroad, a once prosperous Virginia-based line chartered in 1847. In 1880 the R&D's owners organized a holding company with the interminable name Richmond and West Point Terminal Railway and Warehouse Company, or Richmond Terminal for short. The move aimed to foster further expansion, as the R&D's original charter forbade the leasing of any road not directly connected to it. The new company aggressively acquired smaller lines in the South and by 1890 controlled more than 8,000 miles of rail stretching from Washington D.C. to Meridian, Mississippi.

By 1892, however, over-expansion and poor management had left the Richmond Terminal in financial straits. The nationwide depression of 1893 made refinancing difficult, and by the end of the year nearly all of the company's railroads had fallen into receivership. Seventy-four other railroads, many in the South, also went into receivership during the depression. A committee of Richmond Terminal stockholders asked New York financier J. P. Morgan to reorganize the railroad. Morgan agreed, provided that he chose the people to head the new effort.

The man Morgan picked to lead the company was a Confederate veteran and proven railroad man from Georgia named Samuel Spencer. A talented workaholic by today's terms, Spencer impressed his employers with his hard-nosed, business-like approach. Each time he switched companies (a common practice of career railroad men in that era), he moved to a more prominent position. As superintendent of the Long Island Railroad, Spencer attracted the attention of Morgan, who hired him as railroad advisor. Morgan knew that if anyone could make the troubled rail network profitable, it was Spencer.

Morgan decided to reorganize the Richmond Terminal as "The Southern Railway Company." It began operating on July 1, 1894, with

North Carolina Division of Archives and History

Salisbury, N.C., shown here, was an established rail center and junction. Residents hoped to receive the new Southern repair facility.

Spencer as president. Beginning with only 2,000 miles of track from the old Richmond Terminal, Spencer used Morgan's financial backing to snatch up many railroads which formerly had been part of the system. In a few months the Southern Railway grew to 4,392 miles. During its first year the company grossed $17.1 million with profits of $896,000, an astounding feat considering the financial difficulties of the old Richmond Terminal.

Spencer tirelessly expanded Southern's mileage and improved its track and rolling stock. One of the lines which he coveted most was the North Carolina Railroad (NCRR), which formed a crescent across the North Carolina Piedmont from Goldsboro by way of Raleigh and Greensboro to Charlotte. The state had provided three-fourth of the capital to build the road years earlier and was its main stockholder.

Fearing the R&D would build a competing line from Greensboro to Charlotte and siphon off their business, the directors of the NCRR agreed in 1871 to lease their entire line to the R&D for 30 years at $260,000 per year. When Southern replaced the R&D, Samuel Spencer recognized the NCRR's importance as the center of the multi-state system he was building. He offered, and the NCRR accepted, a new 99-year lease to begin January 1, 1896. The lease infuriated Republicans and Populists in the North Carolina legislature who thought the lease rate too low. In 1897 Daniel Russell, the Republican governor of North Carolina, tried to annul the lease. Spencer secured it after months of legal wrangling, but bitterness remained between the railroad and state officials.

Spencer had already acquired the Western North Carolina Railroad (WNCRR), whose main line branched off the NCRR at Salisbury and stretched west toward the Blue Ridge. The WNCRR scaled the mountains via six tunnels and an agonizing sequence of loops before reaching the Tennessee border at Paint Rock. Before its completion the WNCRR became part of the Richmond Terminal, whose directors recognized that such an east/west route could ultimately lead to the Ohio River and the Midwest. This same notion spurred Sam Spencer. In August 1894 Southern bought the bankrupt WNCRR, valued at $17 million, at auction for a mere $500,000. It was one of many deals Spencer arranged; by 1900 he merged 68 railroads into the system using 109 separate charters.

The speedy acquisition of many formerly independent lines left Southern with a problem. Much of its inherited rolling stock badly needed repairs which the company's meager shops could not handle. In the rail-

North Carolina Division of Archives and History

Southern soon needed both new locomotives and shops to repair its aging fleet. Baldwin built 4-6-0 No. 353 for Southern passenger service in 1899. Renumbered as 1054 in 1903, the locomotive was scrapped at Spencer in 1932.

way's first annual report (June 1895), Spencer admitted that the "antiquated and poorly equipped" shops were "not sufficient for their purposes." He reported that shops at Atlanta and Knoxville were being enlarged to handle heavy repairs but added that "one additional large shop may be necessary."

The most pressing need for another shop complex was on the eastern main line between Washington and Atlanta. It was customary in that era for trains to switch locomotives every 150 miles to be refueled, inspected for damage and wear, and repaired as needed. By putting a major terminal and shop facility midway between the two cities with smaller terminals at the quarter marks, Southern could divide the Washington-to-Atlanta run into four segments of about 160 miles each. The large central shops site could be used for light repairs like other terminals but also would be available for complete overhauls and servicing of possible wrecks.

In late 1895 or early 1896 it became public knowledge that Southern was scouting the middle section of the main line for a site to build a shops facility that would bring hundreds of new jobs. Citizens of Charlotte grew excited for their town was located near the midpoint and was the junction of several lines in the Southern system. Surely, the people thought, with its location and large population (compared to nearby towns) Charlotte was the logical choice for the complex.

From Southern's point of view, however, the decision was much more complicated. Company engineers surveyed and decided that Salisbury (about 40 miles northeast of Charlotte) was nearer the midpoint. Salisbury, county seat of Rowan County, had been chartered in 1753 and was one of the older towns in the state. Its growth had been slow, how-

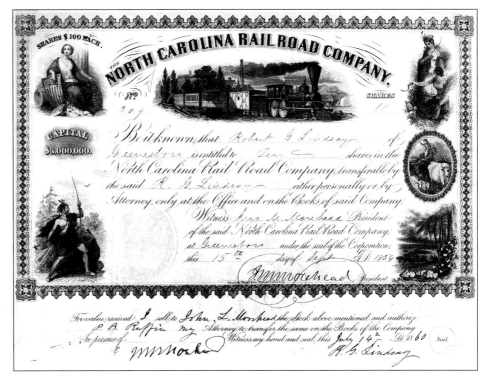

North Carolina Division of Archives and History

The North Carolina Railroad, leased by Southern in 1896, issued this stock certificate in 1854 to Robert G. Lindsay of Greensboro.

ever, due in large part to the agonizingly poor, muddy roads of the colonial and early national periods. Legislators from Rowan County pushed for creation of the North Carolina Railroad, and the people of Salisbury were elated to learn that the railroad would pass through their town. The first trains roared into Salisbury in January 1855, frightening humans and animals alike but bringing hope of economic and industrial growth. The opportunity improved even further when Salisbury became the eastern terminus of the Western North Carolina Railroad, increasing its importance as a rail center.

The promised economic growth was not quick in coming, however. While Charlotte grew rapidly from 1860 to 1890 and several railroads established terminals there, Salisbury attracted no new railroads or large industries and experienced much less growth. An 1887 editorial in *The Charlotte Observer* was condescending. The people of Rowan, it said, had "laid down and slept on their opportunities" and had made little effort to

promote further industrial or railroad development.

At the same time, though, one of Rowan's most prominent citizens was doing all within his power to change this. He was John Steele Henderson, Confederate veteran, lawyer, former state senator, the county's largest landholder, and an ardent supporter of industrial development. In 1884 he was elected to the U.S. House of Representatives for the first of five terms. In the 1894 election he was defeated by a candidate of the short-lived Populist party.

Henderson actually felt some relief in escaping the high-pressure life of a congressman. Yet after living ten years on a congressman's wages, Henderson was worried about his financial future. He still owned a great deal of land and was probably more concerned about maintaining his current standard of living than with becoming impoverished. In letters to his wife Elizabeth in Salisbury he expressed a despondency which bordered on depression. "When my term ends," he lamented, "I will be a statesman out of a job and in search of work."

Henderson unsuccessfully sought employment with the new Southern Railway in Washington. Sometime during his interviews with Southern, Henderson learned that the company planned a new shop complex at or near his hometown of Salisbury. He saw an opportunity to improve his financial status and bring a new industry to Rowan County. In late 1895 Henderson entered into secret negotiations with Southern officials. A savvy real estate speculator before his years in Congress, he put forth the most ambitious land deal of his life. He proposed to buy land secretly for the new shop complex and sell it to the railroad at or near the low price he would pay, thus sparing the railroad the intense publicity of a search for a proper location. Unconfirmed legend has it that Henderson also promised that the Salisbury city limits would never be enlarged to include the site, thus saving the company from paying city taxes. Whatever deal Henderson offered, it lured Southern to Rowan County.

Salisbury also offered Southern officials other advantages. Besides being centrally located on the eastern main line, it was also the point at which the old Western North Carolina Railroad left the main line for Asheville, Knoxville, and beyond. Salisbury was thus the junction of Southern's north/south and east/west lines.

Henderson kept his conferences with the railway a secret from his family and friends in Salisbury. In January 1896 he began buying large tracts of land two miles north of Salisbury directly on Southern's main line. One of his largest purchases was 101.8 acres from an African-American farmer named Robert Partee at $24.50 per acre. He eventually accumulated 162.2 acres at the spot but continued to tell no one what he was

up to. Mrs. Henderson worried that the land buying spree would be the final stage in their financial ruin, but her persistent inquiries went unanswered.

Mrs. Henderson and the people of Salisbury had to wait until February 26 when Southern vice presidents William Baldwin and Col. Alexander Boyd Andrews arrived in town. Colonel Andrews was a Tar Heel and career railroad man who had helped build the Western North Carolina Railroad over the Blue Ridge mountains. He and Baldwin announced that Henderson's land would be the site of a new shop complex which would have a tremendous economic impact on Salisbury and Rowan County. Three days later Elizabeth Henderson accompanied her husband to the Rowan County register of deeds where he sold 141 acres to the railroad at little more than the price he had paid for them.

Mrs. Henderson revealed her husband's plan for the remainder of the land in a letter to her daughter:

"Although you have read the good news you can't appreciate its significance to us. . . . The immense shops are to be located about a mile and three quarters below us and right in the midst of Mr. Henderson's land. A town of several thousand inhabitants is obliged to spring up right there and his land will have to be purchased by the people for their homes. Mr. H is only selling a small amount of his land for the shops… the great advantage is that his land surrounds all this spot.

He has been engaged in this for some time but it was a profound secret. …The people for several weeks have been frantic to find out something—conjectured all sorts of things that he was going to found a colony and different things. …" [A few days later Mrs. Henderson wrote] "the excitement is increasing—There is talk of electric lights or of extending Main Street out to the shops or hav-

ing electric cars… Mr. H has been writing deeds all day. Col. [Andrews] is so exited over his piece of land that he has gotten drunk for two days! We have great expectations but very little money."

That changed before long. Many people who came to work at the shops bought land from Henderson. After the turn of the century he sold more land to the railway for expansion of the shops, but this time for a large profit. By the time he died in 1916 John Steele Henderson was again wealthy.

But in 1896 not everyone was happy that the new shops would be built near Salisbury. The people of Charlotte were shocked. What did little Salisbury, they wondered, possibly have to offer the railway? In March 1896 prominent Charlotteans traveled to Southern headquarters to persuade Samuel Spencer to change his mind and locate the shops in Charlotte. The delegation received a cold reception from Spencer, who reportedly told them: "If you were to give me an iron-clad contract signed by every shipper, big and little, in Charlotte, guaranteeing me all their business for a period of five years, I could not build the shops at Charlotte. The shops are to cost $225,000. If you were to give the land free and build the shops at your own expense, turning them over to us as a present, we could not accept them located at Charlotte." That was the final word. The shops would be located in Rowan County.

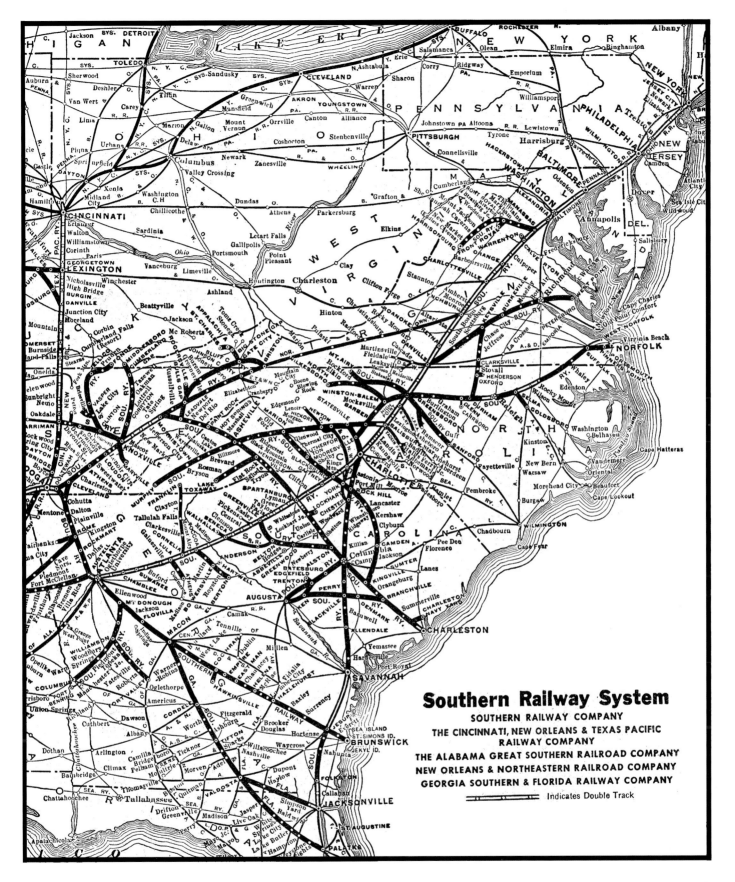

Spencer's central location between Washington, D.C., and Atlanta, Ga., on the Southern's busy main line was a factor in locating the shops there. This map, from a 1950 timetable, shows Charlotte and Salisbury. Spencer is just north of Salisbury, N.C.

For over half a century the strong iron and steel of buildings and steam locomotives made the massive complex built at Spencer the largest employer and pride of Rowan County.

Building the Shops and Town

On March 23, 1896, workmen swarmed over Southern's new land and turned the first shovelfulls of 75,000 cubic yards of earth moved to build the shops in subsequent months. The John S. Pettyjohn and W.W. Dornin companies of Lynchburg, Virginia, were contracted to construct the shop buildings. During the spring and summer the site was a flurry of activity with laborers moving dirt, engineers studying blueprints, masons laying foundations, and construction workers putting together various buildings. Building materials arrived in rail cars via the Southern main line. The larger buildings were designed to be constructed quickly with steel frames resting on substantial masonry. Workmen covered the frames with corrugated steel siding and slate roofs.

Curious townspeople ventured out each day to observe the progress.

They learned that Southern planned to add terminal facilities including a freight classification yard, livestock pens, and a coaling plant.

On August 19, less than five months later, the shops began operating with Samuel Spencer presiding at opening ceremonies. The shops were named for Spencer, though it is not known who in the company was responsible for this. It seems unlikely that a man as practical and self-effacing as Spencer would have named the shops after himself.

The original buildings included a roundhouse, machine shop, combination smith and boiler shop, woodworking shop, storehouse/office building, power plant, and car repair shed.

The roundhouse had 15 stalls, each 70 feet deep. The rails in each stall were just under 60 feet long, leaving space for workmen and equipment

to move around the locomotives. Each stall had a "smokejack" in the roof to allow smoke from locomotives to escape from the building. At least one stall had a pit for dropping locomotive and tender wheels. Twenty-five uncovered tracks also radiated out from the turntable opposite the roundhouse. Ten of these were equipped with air, water, and steam pipes for washing out locomotive boilers. The 60-foot turntable was made largely of wood and iron. It appears to have been pushed around manually by bars which stuck out each end.

In accord with standard shop layout of the era, the machine shop was behind the roundhouse, allowing easy access between the two buildings. Locomotives needing heavy repair were pushed into one of ten stalls which stretched 35 feet into the building. Only locomotives needing

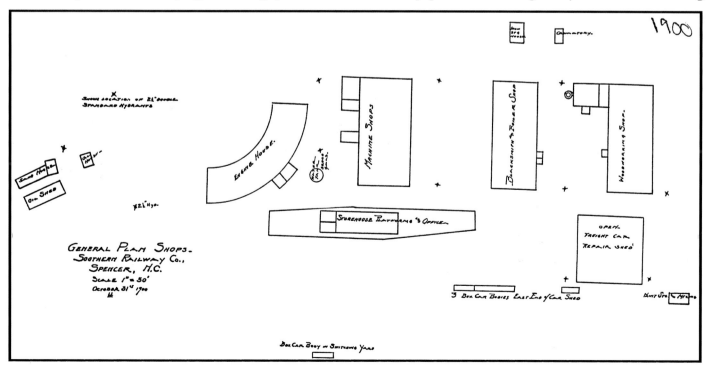

North Carolina Division of Archives and History
An early Southern drawing shows the original shop buildings.

SOUTHERN RAILWAY ROUND HOUSE, SPENCER, NEAR SALISBURY, N. C.

North Carolina Division of Archives and History

This 1910 postcard reveals the 1896 roundhouse, sand house (center), and other buildings.

major repairs or overhaul entered the machine shop. All other repair was handled in the roundhouse. Shopmen working in the machine shop could perform six to eight complete overhauls per month.

Many of the machine tools used in this and other buildings had been consolidated from smaller shops at railroads purchased by Southern. The old Western North Carolina Railroad shops in Salisbury and the North Carolina Railroad shops in Burlington (once known as "Company Shops") were primary sources of machines. Craftsmen in these shops were likewise transferred to the new facility. Southern also spared no expense for new, modern turret lathes, milling machines, bolt cutters, and other machines needed to repair parts or make hand tools.

Blacksmithing and boiler repair were in a similar building penetrated by three tracks. These tracks joined those which ran into the machine shop by way of a 40-foot transfer table which moved longitudinally along a 225-foot runway between the buildings. The transfer table was used to move locomotives into the machine shop and transfer parts and machinery between it and the smith/boiler shop.

North of the smith/boiler shop was the woodworking shop, where wood used in freight car and locomotive cab repair was planed and cut to size. Logs from western North Carolina were brought to the shop on flatbed cars pushed directly into the building and unloaded. The woodworking shop was beside the car repair shed so the cut wood could be easily transferred to the shed. Within a few years the woodworking shop produced over 400,000 board feet of lumber monthly.

The car repair shed was open at each end to allow through passage of six tracks which led directly from the freight yard to the shed. In the yard, inspectors identified cars needing repairs, and these were lined up on the six tracks. Car repairmen, called "car knockers" by other shopmen because of their incessant hammering on the wooden cars, could perform almost any repair on freight or passenger cars and could have built a wooden boxcar from scratch. In the first years of the shops, the carmen repaired as many as 150 cars per day.

A storehouse/office building was constructed south of the car repair sheds and beside the machine shop. The master mechanic, the highest

ranking manager at the site, kept his office in the building and was joined by payroll clerks, typists, and telephone operators. Anything shopworkers needed in their work from spare parts to tools to office supplies resided in the storehouse. Supplies were brought to the site in rail cars. The materials were first unloaded onto concrete platforms extending 150 feet north and 100 feet south of the building. At the north end workers later built a small building only eight feet square in which they stored gunpowder, dynamite, railroad torpedoes, and fuses.

A power plant, often referred to as the boiler house or powerhouse, was next to the woodworking shop and supplied steam, electricity, and heat to the other buildings. Four 100-horsepower, coal-fired boilers created the heat and steam. Generators turned by steam produced electricity for exterior and interior lighting at the shops. An 85-foot-tall smokestack supplied draft for the coal fires under the boilers. During construction of the shops some workers had taken bad falls building the smokestack, and the men were relieved when it was completed. They celebrated by unfurling an American flag from the top of the smokestack but were ordered to take it down a few days later. The railway official who gave the order was an Englishman who was not impressed with the workers' patriotic fervor.

Minor buildings also present when the shops opened in 1896 included iron, paint, and oil storage sheds and a crematory for disposal of dead or diseased animals from the stockyards.

Plentiful fresh water is essential to the operation of any shops, and at Spencer it was stored originally in a 60,000-gallon tank atop a 60-foot tower behind the roundhouse. The water was available to fight fires but was used every day to wash out and refill boilers of locomotives being serviced in the roundhouse. Water also was used in the powerhouse boilers, for drinking, and for cleaning dirty shop workers at the end of the day. The water came from the Yadkin River, over three miles north of the shops. Southern built a pump station at the river which, in later years, drew six million gallons of water per day. To handle this enormous flow several storage tanks were added at the shops and along the route of the pipeline from the pump station to the shops.

The freight yard and terminal facilities built adjacent to the shops were also named for Samuel Spencer and played a vital role in movement of traffic along Southern's eastern lines. The freight yard opened with 11 tracks operational, but others were added later. Rail cars were sorted on these tracks by gravity. A car would be nudged by a switch engine to get it rolling to the proper track and be stopped there by a brakeman. Train crews picked up orders at the yard office next to the main line tracks. All freight trains which came through the yard stopped to switch locomotives and crews even if they had no cars to deposit or take on. Passenger trains switched locomotives and crews at the Salisbury or Spencer depots.

Terminal facilities included a trestle coaling station which local newspapers hailed as the "world's largest." The trestle built over the coal storage bin was 20 feet high and 700 feet long. The bin, 700 feet long and 70 feet wide, held 15,000 tons of coal. Gondola cars of coal were pushed onto the trestle by a switch engine. Once the cars were over the bin, their bottoms or sides swung out like trap doors, and coal fell into the bin. Locomotive tenders to be loaded with coal sat on tracks 14 feet lower than and beside the coal bin. Iron chutes on the bin were lowered by chain hoists, and the coal poured into the tenders. More than 70 tenders per day were loaded in this way.

ROUND HOUSE. SOUTHERN R. R. SHOPS, Spencer, N. C.

North Carolina Division of Archives and History

In this early postcard view locomotives rest on some of the 25 tracks surrounding the turntable at the 1896 roundhouse (right).

Adjacent to the coal bin was a cinder pit where clinkers, unburned coal ashes from locomotive fireboxes, were dumped after the fires had been extinguished, or "killed." The fire was killed in almost every locomotive which came onto the site for inspection and repair, so there was usually plenty of activity around the pit. The "pit" was actually a sloping platform under and beside the tracks holding locomotives. Cinders were scraped and washed from the ash pans of the locomotives onto the platform and then shoveled into gondola cars on an adjacent track eight feet below the platform.

At the coaling plant and cinder pit workers pushed wheelbarrows and shoveled and scraped coal and cinders into rail cars, platforms, and chutes. This back-breaking work was mostly done by African-Americans who were fully exposed to the elements while working and endured periods of intense boredom followed by frantic activity. Sometimes men broke under the pressure. One night in May 1907

David Driscoll/SRHA collection

This afternoon view of the Spencer depot in March 1947 shows the small wood depot actually located on the East Spencer side of the yard at the north end of the facility.

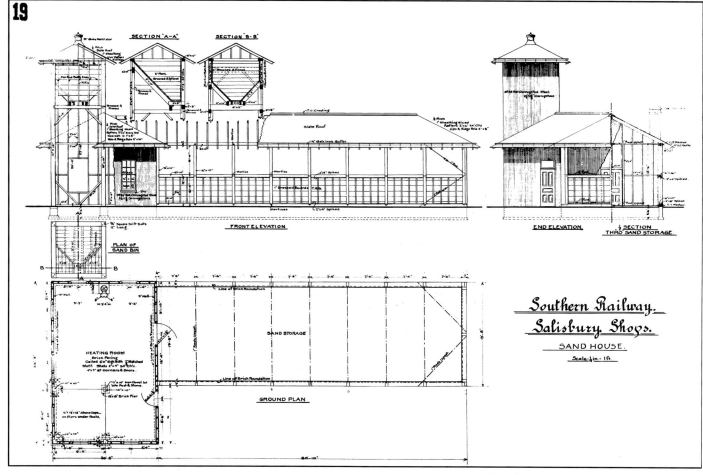

SECTION "A-A"   SECTION "B-B"

FRONT ELEVATION

PLAN OF
SAND BIN

END ELEVATION   ½ SECTION
THRO SAND STORAGE

HEATING ROOM

SAND STORAGE

GROUND PLAN

Southern Railway.
Salisbury Shops.
SAND HOUSE.
Scale: ½ in = 1 ft

This typical Southern drawing depicts the 1896 sand house.

there was little work to be done at the cinder pit, and a laborer named George Fox fell asleep in a chair beside the pit. A fellow worker, Fred Muse, conceived what he thought to be a humorous method of waking Fox. He set fire to an oily rag and held it under Fox's nose. Fox awoke with a start, and the other workers hooted with laughter. Fox, however, was furious. After a shouting match with Muse, he threw down his shovel and marched to his home not far from the Spencer yards. He seized a revolver, walked calmly back to the cinder pits, and pointed it at Muse, who began to realize that his joke was not so funny after all. Fox pulled the trigger four times; three bullets found Muse, who died instantly. "Damn you, I guess you're dead now," Fox exclaimed and lit a cigarette. Fox made no attempt to leave until told that the police had been called. He then tried to walk

away but was detained by fellow workers and a locomotive engineer attracted to the commotion. Soon the chief of police arrived and carried him to jail. This was an isolated incident! Work at the cinder pits was usually not so exciting or dangerous.

Just north of the coal bin and cinder pits was the sand house where sand used by locomotives for added traction was dried and stored. Use of sand for traction began in Pennsylvania in 1836 during a grasshopper plague. Many of the insects were squashed by locomotive wheels, making the rails too slippery for the wheels to get a proper grip. Someone found that pouring sand on the rails provided traction, and primitive sand boxes were installed on locomotives. It was not long before the practice became standard on all railroads. By the time Spencer Shops opened, most locomotives had a "sand

dome" at the top of the locomotive in front of the cab. If the engineer encountered slippery rails, he turned a valve which allowed sand from the dome to travel down the locomotive's body through narrow piping to the tracks in front of the wheels. On most locomotives the sand moved by gravity and air pressure, and it had to be dried thoroughly so as not to become stuck in the pipe.

Sand for Spencer came from the Yadkin River in gondola cars and was unloaded into the storage section of the sand house. In the original building the sand was dried using a stove, though the exact method is unknown. In those early years dried sand was usually poured into locomotive sand domes one bucket at a time.

Another important complex adjacent to the Spencer yard was the stockyards, or "cattle pens" as they were known locally. Before the advent

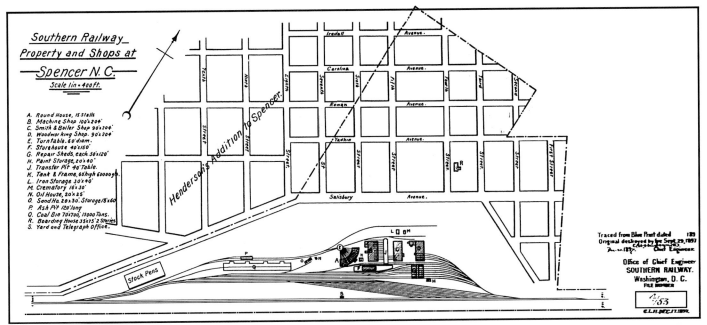

Southern Railway
Property and Shops at
Spencer N.C.
Scale 1 in = 400 ft.

A. Round House, 15 Stalls
B. Machine Shop 100'x204'
C. Smith & Boiler Shop 90'x204'
D. Woodworking Shop 90'x204'
E. Turntable 60'diam.
F. Storehouse 40'x150'
G. Repair Sheds, each 50'x120'
H. Paint Storage 20'x40'
J. Transfer Pit 40'Table.
K. Tank & Frame 60'high 6000009.
L. Iron Storage 30'x40'
M. Crematory 16'x30'
N. Oil House 20'x25'
O. Sand Ho. 20'x30' Storage 18'x60'
P. Ash Pit 120'long
Q. Coal Bin 70'x700, 15000 Tons.
R. Boarding House 35'x75' 2 Stories
S. Yard and Telegraph Office.

Henderson's Addition to Spencer

Iredell Avenue
Carolina Avenue
Rowan Avenue
Yadkin Avenue
Salisbury Avenue

Stock Pens

Traced from Blue Print dated 189
Original destroyed by fire Sept 29, 1897

Office of Chief Engineer
SOUTHERN RAILWAY.
Washington, D.C.
FILE NUMBER

North Carolina Division of Archives and History

The railroad developed its property adjacent to the shops into the town of Spencer.

---

of refrigerated boxcars for hauling meat, live cattle and hogs were carried on freight trains. From farms in the Deep South and Southwest, the animals traveled to slaughterhouses in northern cities. Shortly after 1880 a new federal law forbade movement of livestock by rail for more than 28 hours without a five-hour stop to feed and rest the animals. Selling of livestock by the pound was further incentive for railroads to allow animals to eat. Any weight lost in transit lessened their value at the slaughterhouses.

To comply with the federal rulings railroads established areas at major rail terminals where animals could be unloaded, fed, watered, and rested. The original Spencer stockyards included three single-deck and two double-deck chutes for loading and unloading animals. There were 20 livestock pens and seven quarantine pens, each able to hold one carload of livestock. The pens kept animals with actual or likely infections or disease separate from healthy animals. By 1899 Spencer reportedly had one of the largest stock pens in the Southern system.

Development of the Town of Spencer

The tremendous size and scope of the Spencer Shops and terminal demanded a small army of workers. Skilled craftsmen at many smaller shops on Southern's eastern lines were transferred to the new shops. Many came from the old North Carolina Railroad shops in Burlington or from shops in Charlotte and upper South Carolina. Because trains changed crews at the Spencer terminal, engineers, firemen, brakemen, and conductors also descended on the area. These men brought families and intended to settle down and make new homes. Some chose Salisbury or rural sections of Rowan County, but most wanted to live close to their workplace. Traditionally railroads had built communities for workers near their new shops. Elizabeth Henderson's reference to a "separate town" in February 1896 revealed that Southern had planned from the beginning to establish such a community.

During the summer of 1896, as construction continued on the shops, Southern began to partition 84.9 acres of nearby land into 500 lots. Streets were numbered or named for local geographic features or historical figures. On May 3, 1897, the railway

"sold" this land for one dollar to Alexander Boyd Andrews Jr., a 24-year-old Raleigh lawyer and son of the line's vice-president. Young Andrews settled in Raleigh about that time. As trustee for Southern, Andrews signed as grantor (seller) on all deeds for Spencer lots though he lived over 100 miles away.

Lots for homes and businesses sold for $100 apiece, and it was not uncommon for two or more lots to be sold to the same person. The lots were relatively small, 50 by 145 feet for dwelling lots and 25 by 145 feet for those designated for businesses.

Residential deeds contained a number of restrictive covenants. Within a year from the purchase a dwelling had to be constructed costing not less than $400 and approved by an architect appointed by Andrews. The front facade of the building was to be at least 20 feet from the street. Only one dwelling could be built on each lot, but a "tenement" for a full-time servant was allowed. A stable and out buildings were also allowed, but could be no closer than 60 feet to the street. No alcohol could be sold on the premises. Any "privy vault" had to be watertight, and all sewage was to be disposed to a safe distance by sub-surface irrigation until a public sewer system

11

North Carolina Division of Archives and History

Spencer grew quickly into a substantial town with sidewalks preceding paved streets.

could be built. These restrictions aided public health and aesthetic standards for the community.

Andrews did not place restrictions on commercial buildings, but there were restrictions on property that Southern donated, through him, to religious organizations. A building approved by his architect and costing no less than $2000 had to be built within one year. The building could be used for religious purposes only, and no liquor could be served.

At no point did Southern require employees to buy these lots, and non-employees apparently had an equal opportunity to buy them. While Southern did create moral and aesthetic standards through deed restrictions, it provided lots strictly as a service for employees who wished to live there.

The railway also had no pretense of monopolizing land near the shops as the small size (84 acres) of its planned community indicates. The shops and land sold to Andrews were surrounded by private plots. Their owners were entrepreneurs who no doubt realized a profit by developing other subdivisions for shop workers. The communities of Newton Heights, Elizabeth Heights (owned by John Steele Henderson), and Oakland Park were eventually created around the land owned by Andrews. About the time that the shops opened, the growing community also assumed the name Spencer.

Train crews arriving at the freight yard from other towns had a layover of eight hours or less before they could begin their next run. The railway and several entrepreneurs built boarding houses in Spencer for the trainmen. The boarding houses were also useful to relocated men from Burlington who had left their families behind. They could stay in the boarding houses during the week and return home on weekends. In 1901 the railroad helped establish a YMCA in a rented house. The building had a few bedrooms, but the bathroom, with its twin tubs, was the favorite room of tired and dirty trainmen. Absence of indoor plumbing was overcome by filling the tubs with water pumped from a well and heated by a boiler. The water escaped into a ditch under the building.

In 1901 the 625 residents of Spencer were granted incorporation by the state legislature. The new town's boundaries did not include any part of the shops or freight yard. A special clause stipulated that a portion of the unsold Andrews land across the street from the shops could not be taxed. Except that its property would not be taxed by the new town, the railway appears to have had little influence on Spencer's incorporation. The development of the shops also helped foster creation of another town.

Directly across the main line tracks from the shops, a community developed at nearly the same rate as Spencer but under no influence from the railroad. In 1896 several boarding houses were built across the tracks followed by a number of smaller, private houses. About that time George M. Isenhour of Pennsylvania established a brick plant on the east side of the tracks and began supplying brick for construction of the shops. Many people moved to the area to work at the brick plant (which remains in operation to this day) or the shops, creating a real estate boom similar to that of Spencer. People began referring to the eastern community as Southern City.

Residents of Southern City also applied for incorporation in 1901 and asked that their town be called East Spencer. The name change probably reflects the common sense of history and purpose of people in both communities.

East Spencer's independence from the railway affected it in several ways. A haphazard layout of streets emerged in contrast to the gridiron pattern designed by Southern engineers for Spencer. Henderson, who owned much of the land that became East Spencer, put no restriction on lots he sold which resulted in a more random placement of dwellings. The railway could not offer free land for churches, and several congregations eventually moved to Spencer for that benefit. The shops' fire department serviced Spencer, but East Spencer lacked fire protection until 1910.

It is significant that Southern allowed development of a totally independent community adjacent to its shops. The lack of control over both Spencer and East Spencer contrasts with procedures of other railroads. Some companies sought to establish control of the entire adjacent areas and also looked to extend hegemony over

East Spencer (foreground), shown in the late 1940s, developed across the Southern main line from the town of Spencer.

many aspects of employees' daily lives. These were true "railroad towns," and clearly Spencer does not quite fit this mold. One historian states that a railroad town "must depend directly on the railroad not only for its creation and its current prosperity, but also for its mental, cultural, and spiritual existence," and cites Altoona, Pennsylvania, as a perfect example. Streets and lots of Altoona, as at Spencer, were laid out by railroad draftsmen. The dwellings at Altoona, however, were very close to each other and the shops. The houses, except for those of company officers, had a "dull, drab" sameness, which helped leave the impression that the town was "deadly uninteresting."

While earlier dwellings at Spencer were often comparable to each other in design, this appears to have been due to the similar economic situations of Spencer families (almost all were middle class) and the need for hasty, simple construction

due to the many transfers of employees from other shop sites. The restrictive covenants created a sense of space between the houses, and a wide street, Salisbury Avenue, separated the town from the shops.

Another example of a shops community controlled by the railroad was Company Shops, established in Alamance County by the North Carolina Railroad Company in the 1850s. Company president Charles F. Fisher intended that the railroad own all the land "to give the Company that territorial jurisdiction essential to the proper police regulation of the Machine Shops." Boarding houses for employees were built in rows adjacent to the shops. In contrast, fine, two-story houses for company officials were built across the main line from the shop buildings to reduce exposure to noise. A commissary and civic building were erected. No outside businesses were allowed on company property. With these devices, the

North Carolina Railroad attempted to make the town self-sufficient but also dependent upon company control.

It seems easy to imagine that Southern could have followed the precedent of Altoona or Company Shops at Spencer. Instead the railroad bypassed the stage of development where employees were sheltered only in boarding houses. From the beginning the company sold land for private dwellings, with restrictive covenants added to create some control over development. In contrast to the initial stages of Company Shops, private business was encouraged at Spencer. Southern did contract the Sands Company to provide a "company store," but shop workers certainly were not limited to making all their purchases there. The railroad soon had plenty to do to operate and expand the shops to service an upgraded locomotive fleet without also running a company town.

Locomotives rest in various states of disassembly during overhaul in the back shop.

Early Growth of the Shops
1900-1918

3

Under the skilled leadership of Samuel Spencer the Southern grew dramatically in its first ten years. Spencer worked tirelessly to make his company a respected competitor in the booming railroad industry. He missed Christmas and other holidays with his family because he believed he could not afford to take any time off.

While working to strengthen his own company, Spencer kept a close eye on its regional rivals, the Atlantic Coast Line, Seaboard Air Line, and Louisville and Nashville railroads. Formed a few years before the Southern, these companies also were created by northern financiers trying to link financially insecure southern railroads into profitable systems. By 1900 the Atlantic Coast Line and the Seaboard had built roughly parallel systems from Virginia to Florida. Both growing companies had over 2,000 miles of track. They would be rivals until they merged into the Seaboard Coast Line in 1967. In 1900 the Louisville & Nashville had nearly 5,000 miles of track from Illinois to the Gulf Coast and branched into seven southern states.

In spite of such success, Southern accumulated mileage and traffic at a faster rate. By 1900 the system contained 7,200 miles of track from Washington to Mississippi and from the Ohio River to Florida. In just five years freight traffic had doubled and passenger traffic had increased 85 percent.

But Samuel Spencer knew that thousands of miles of track and a busy

schedule were useless without strong, quick locomotives. He discovered the locomotives the Southern had inherited were inadequate, many ready for the scrap heap. Most were stubby Americans (4-4-0) or Moguls (2-6-0) with inadequate power for the mountainous regions of his system. New locomotives were in order, and in 1897 Spencer purchased the first of

CAR SHOP. SOUTHERN R. R. SHOPS, Spencer, N. C.

North Carolina Division of Archives and History

The massive back shop, some 600 feet long and 150 feet wide, was one of the largest industrial buildings in the state when completed in 1905.

750 Consolidation (2-8-0) locomotives the company would obtain by 1912. The Consolidations, while not large, were deceptively strong and agile and became the most common locomotive on the Southern and in America. Spencer also invested in powerful Pacifics (4-6-2) to haul passenger trains over the mountainous Asheville Division which joined the main line near Spencer.

These new and larger locomotives had profound consequences for Spencer Shops. Southern officials quickly recognized that the roundhouse and machine shop, while just a few years old, were too small. The original machine shop, with its ten 35-foot repair stalls, was the most obsolete.

By the spring of 1904 Southern's chief engineers and the Spencer master mechanic, S. R. Richards, had designed a new facility to triple maintenance and repair capacity. The new building, a combination machine and erecting shop, would resemble in appearance and function a locomotive factory. The original machine shop at Spencer had a transverse design with tracks inside the shop perpendicular to its length. The new building would have a longitudinal design in which tracks ran through it lengthwise. Instead of tearing down the old buildings, the engineers decided to keep them in use. This, combined with the narrowness of the shop property, made a longitudinal building the most logical choice. It would fit snugly just east of the existing buildings, making transfer of parts between them easier.

Southern called the John P. Pettyjohn Company of Lynchburg, Virginia, builder of the original shops, to erect the new building. Work began in the spring of 1904 and was completed by January 1905. The massive building measured 596'2" long, 150' wide, and 64'2" tall. It dwarfed every other building in Rowan County. Its frame consisted of steel columns and roof trusses built by the American Bridge Company. About 40 percent of the wall and roof area was glass to let in natural light. For the walls Southern bought 2,500,000 bricks from the nearby Isenhour Brick

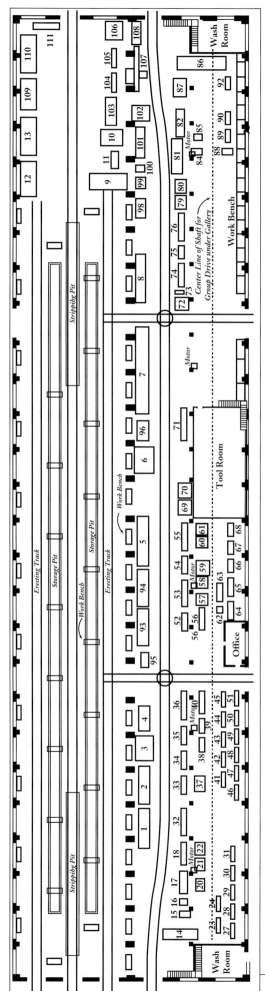

Machines Driven By Individual Motors

No. of Mach.	Kind	Size
1	Planer	48" x 48" x 10'
2	Planer	18" x 36" x 10'
3	Radial drill	7' arm
4	Double-head shaper	24"
5	Planer	48" x 48" x 15'
6	Radial Drill	7' arm
7	Planer	48" x 48" x 26'
8	Milling Machine	30" x 30" x 14'
9	Planer	60" x 60" x 10'
10	Slotter	26"
11	Lathe	42" x 72"
12	Driving Wheel Lathe	90"
13	Driving Wheel Lathe	90"

Machines Driven in Groups

No.	Kind	Size
14	Planer	36" x 36" x 10'
15	Shaper	20"
16	Tool Grinder	---
17	Horiz. Boring Mill	60"
18	Lathe	30" x 84"
19	Turret lathe	2" x 24"
20	Slotter	12"
21	Drill press	36"
22	Drill press	36"
23	Lathe	22" x 84"
24	Lathe	16" x 48"
25	Turret lathe	16" x 36"
26	Turret lathe	16" x 36"
27	Turret lathe	16" x 36"
28	Turret lathe	16" x 36"
29	Turret lathe	16" x 36"
30	Turret lathe	16" x 36"
31	Turret lathe	16" x 36"

Group No. 2

No.	Kind	Size
32	Lathe	30" x 132"
33	Lathe	30" x 72"
34	Lathe	30" x 72"
35	Lathe	30" x 72"
36	Lathe	30" x 132"
37	Shaper	20"
38	Lathe	22" x 48"
39	Lathe	22" x 48"
40	Lathe	20" x 90"
41	Lathe	18" x 48"
42	Lathe	18" x 48"
43	Lathe	18" x 48"
44	Lathe	18" x 48"
45	Lathe	18" x 48"
46	Lathe	16" x 36"
47	Lathe	16" x 36"
48	Lathe	16" x 36"
49	Lathe	16" x 36"
50	Lathe	16" x 36"
51	Lathe	16" x 36"

Group No. 3

No.	Kind	Size
52	Piston Rode Grinder	
53	Lathe	50" x 96"
54	Lathe	36" x 72"
55	Lathe	36" x 132"
56	Lathe	24" x 102"
57	Shaper	20"
58	Drill Press	40"
59	Drill Press	36"
60	Drill Press	40"
61	Drill Press	40"
62	Tool Grinder	---
63	Lathe	22" x 84"
64	Lathe	16" x 84"
65	Lathe	16" x 84"
66	Lathe	16" x 54"
67	Lathe	16" x 54"
68	Lathe	16" x 54"

Group No. 4

No.	Kind	Size
69	Verticle boring mill	51"
70	Verticle boring mill	51"
71	Turret lathe	4 1/4" x 34"
72	Drill press	42"
73	Red bushing press - 2 inch	
74	Lathe	26" x 90"
75	Lathe	26" x 54"
76	Turret lathe	4 3/4" x 24"
	Machines in tool room	10

Group No. 5

No.	Kind	Size
79	Drill Press	13"
80	Drill Press	42"
81	Planer	36" x 36" x 10'
82	Horiz. boring mill	---
84	Shaper	20"
85	Tool grinder	---
86	Planer	48" x 36" x 6'
87	Shaper	18"
88	Shaper	20"
89	Lathe	18" x 54"
90	Lathe	18" x 54"
91	Lathe	26" x 48"
92	Piston rod keyway	---
	Cutter	---

Group No. 6

No.	Kind	Size
93	Planer	36" x 36" x 10'
94	Planer	36" x 36" x 10'
95	Cold Saw	---
96	Slotter	20"

Group No. 7

No.	Kind	Size
98	Vert. milling machine	20"
99	Vert. boring machine	37"
100	Tool grinder	---
101	Lathe	42" x 144"
102	Radial drill	5' 6" arm
103	Milling machine	26" x 26" x 9'

Group No. 8

No.	Kind	Size
104	Lathe	30" x 84"
105	Lathe	30" x 84"
106	Vert. boring mill	84"
107	Cylinder planer	---
108	Cylinder borer	---

Group No. 9

No.	Kind	Size
109	Driving Wheel Lathe	78"
110	Driving Wheel Lathe	78"
111	Driving Wheel Press	---

Machines In Smith Shop

No.	Kind
1	2 inch bolt header (new)
2	Bolt cutter (old)
3	Bolt cutter (old)
4	Bolt shear (old)
5	6-spindle nut tapper
6	Punch and shear (new)
7	3 1/2 inch bolt shear (new)
8	200-lb. Bradley compact hammer (new)
9	1,000 lb. steam hammer (new)
10	Trip hammer (new)
11	Morgan steam hammer (old)
12	Beament steam hammer (old)
13	75-lb. hammer (new)
14	3,000 lb. steam hammer (new)

The *Railroad Gazette* in late 1904 described in detail the arrangement of 111 machines in the back shop.

Company at $5.00 per thousand.

Most of the building's exterior was done by October 1904, and Southern began installing new machines and equipment. Total costs including machinery and equipment exceeded $483,000 (or eight million 1995 dollars). Repair and overhaul work began in the building in January 1905.

The new building was called the "back shop" by Spencer workers. Nineteenth-century railroad men had originated the term to describe heavy repair plants built behind or "out back" of roundhouses. The nickname stuck to the Spencer machine/erecting shop, and it is known as the back shop even today.

The west half of the back shop contained the erecting shop and the east half the machine shop. A "communication track," on which locomotives entered and exited the building, ran the length of the erecting shop. The track was flanked on either side by storage pits, four feet wide and four feet deep, for parts removed from locomotives during overhaul. Erecting tracks, on which locomotives were stripped of parts and reassembled, ran outside the storage pits for 480 feet. Two 60-ton capacity, overhead cranes, to lift and carry locomotives from the communication track to an erecting track, ran the length of the erecting shop. Moving locomotives with these cranes took a great deal of skill. In 1906 an operator dropped a large locomotive several feet to the floor. The crash resounded throughout the shops, but no workers were injured, and the locomotive received only minor damage. An additional 90-ton crane was installed in the 1920s to move new, heavier locomotives.

Heavy machines for re-surfacing locomotive driving wheels sat at the north end of the shop where the erecting tracks ended. The other machine tools occupied much floor space in the machine shop side of the building. A standard gauge track for moving parts and tools on flange-wheeled dollies ran through the center of the machine shop. At two points tracks ran out of the back shop to the woodworking, boiler, and blacksmith shops. The dollies, which carried items between the buildings, could run on all tracks inside or outside the back shop because of mini-turntables located where the tracks crossed.

The concrete floor of the machine and erecting shops was originally brick. This floor tended to cause dust and cracked easily if heavy parts or tools were dropped on it. After a few years the clay bricks were replaced with wooden bricks covered with waste oil to fill in the cracks. The wooden bricks absorbed oil and grease, alleviating the danger of slick spots. Unlike concrete, the wood

absorbed the impact of parts which fell on the floor, reducing damage to both the floor and dropped objects.

A 36-foot-wide gallery ran the length of the back shop 19 feet above the machine shop floor. The gallery contained several small shops where brass, tin, bells, gauges, injectors, lubricators, air pumps, headlights, and turbo-generators were repaired. The gallery also housed the blowers of the building's Sturtevant heating system, which used steam piped from the nearby powerhouse.

Two cranes, one of five-ton and the other of ten-ton capacity, ran the length of the machine shop. The cranes carried parts anywhere in the shop or lifted them up to the gallery. Locker rooms occupied the eastern corners of the shop on the ground and gallery levels.

To supplement ample natural light, a row of 13 Toerring arc lights on each side of the building hung 40 feet above the floor. Workmen cleaned light housings and changed bulbs from the traveling overhead cranes—a job not for the faint of heart.

More than 100 machines were scattered about the machine shop. The majority were lathes, boring mills, grinders, shapers, milling machines, and planers which allowed

shopmen to re-surface worn metal parts or create new parts and tools out of raw material. Most of the machines were powered by overhead shafting, a series of leather belts connecting the machines to electric motors. In the machine shop, several 20-horsepower direct current motors were mounted to the columns at the edge of the gallery. The belts connected the motors to pulleys on the underside of the gallery and connected the pulleys to the machines. The motors turned the shafting, thus rotating the pulleys and ultimately the moving parts of the machines.

Shafting allowed the motors to power one or more machine tools at the same time. The speed at which a machine turned was controlled by where the shafting was attached to a spindle on the side of the machine. The spindle grew smaller in diameter as it moved away from the machine. Changing speeds was much like changing gears on a bicycle in which the chain moves from one sized gear to another on the rear wheel. Shopmen placed sticks under the belt and moved it along the spindle.

The moving belts, generally not covered, were a safety hazard if they broke or workers got too close to them. On occasion men were caught in the belts and flung violently to the

Kenneth L. Miller

This end view of the back shop is based on a drawing from the *Railroad Gazette* article of November 25, 1904.

Interior Machine Building.　SPENCER, N. C.

North Carolina Division of Archives and History

Locomotives stand lined up for overhaul inside the back shop. Note the natural light from windows and skylights.

floor or ceiling. Machines with individual motors gradually replaced belt-driven machines, and by the mid-1940s very few were left.

Completion of the back shop in 1905 led to a game of musical chairs among the shop buildings. Machines and equipment left the original machine shop for the back shop. Boiler, painting, and locomotive cab work moved into the former old building. The blacksmiths stayed in the original boiler/smith shop and received new equipment including forging machines and steam-powered trip hammers. The old transfer table remained in use, shuttling rail cars loaded with parts and supplies into the two buildings.

Completion of the back shop and expansion of the blacksmith shop increased demands on the power plant. The result was an addition to the powerhouse for three new boilers, another 85-foot smokestack, and two steam engines which turned two 200-kilowatt Westinghouse generators. W. S. Sweet, chief shop electrician, expected the increased power output to meet energy needs of any future expansion. He had to add another boiler within two years, however, and his successors expanded the power-house again in 1926 to supply energy for a new roundhouse. Sweet was nei-

ther the first nor last person to underestimate the shops' voracious appetite for energy.

The new back shop and related expansion made Spencer Shops the largest shops on the Southern Railway. They were the primary shops for all company lines east of the Appalachians. The western lines were served by older shops at Knoxville and Chattanooga, expanded in 1896. The Knoxville shops received their own large back shop in 1907. But Spencer remained the Southern's center for experimentation and invention in shop equipment and procedure.

The Spencer freight yard also grew to become one of the largest in the Southern system and the major main-line terminal between Washington and Atlanta. By the 1930s nearly 1800 freight trains would be handled at the yard monthly and 800 passenger trains would visit the Spencer and Salisbury depots. The yard contained nearly 46 miles of track where cars were sorted among trains bound for all parts of the United States. The freight yard was a shifting, groaning mass of rail cars of all shapes and sizes. At all hours of the day and night the metallic clank of couplers being joined and the chugging rumble of switch engines resounded through the well-lit yards.

Larger railroad companies often located less-than-carload freight transfer facilities near major terminals. At such facilities freight was sorted among boxcars according to kind and destination. For example, a carload of chairs from a furniture factory would be broken down and distributed among cars bound for various towns and cities. Transfer facilities were essential to popular mail-order catalogs of the era such as Sears and Roebuck, Montgomery Ward, and Marshall Fields. These companies sent full boxcars to regional transfer facilities where the contents were distributed among cars bound for all towns in that region.

Spencer's location near the junction of Southern's north-south and east-west main lines and the presence of the vast shops and terminals influenced the company's decision to build a transfer facility there in 1907. The facility, known locally as the "transfer sheds," opened November 1 about a mile south of the shops near the Spencer-Salisbury boundary. The complex initially had four sheds 641 feet long and a fifth 950 feet long. Ten tracks ran between the sheds. By the 1920s, when another shed had been added, up to 250 freight cars could be parked between the sheds. The Spencer transfer handled 600,000 tons of freight annually by then with 250 to 300 employees. It was said to be the largest such facility in the Southern system.

The transfer operated eight hours each weekday. In the morning switch engines pushed boxcars onto the tracks between the sheds. Workers then laid wooden bridges between the cars, connecting the sheds so that freight could be transported over the entire complex. The cars were numbered to avoid confusion. The position and destination of each car was carefully noted, so that employees trucking items through the maze of sheds and bridges would know exactly where to go. Workers were either packers or drivers. Packers loaded and unloaded freight from the boxcars. Drivers transported freight between cars with hand-trucks, forklifts, or small tractors. Once freight had been distributed, the planks were taken up and the cars pushed out of the sheds. The packed cars had been lined up with eastbound cars on one track, northbound cars on another, and so forth. At the lunch hour and at the end of the day, loaded cars were pushed to the freight yard to be coupled to departing trains.

Though technically not part of Spencer Shops, the transfer sheds brought the area recognition as a rail center and had a positive economic impact on the county, especially among the unskilled or under-educated. Most of the shed workers were African-Americans who for many years had few opportunities in local industries such as cotton mills. Pay at the sheds was significantly less than for skilled shop workers but more than most blacks could make farming or in the few laborer jobs they could find in the county. The sheds also provided jobs for college and high school students during summer months when freight traffic was heavier. Many men who were laid-off at the shops also worked at the sheds until called back.

After the transfer sheds opened in 1907, Southern wanted to increase Spencer's shops and yards even more, but a nationwide economic recession that fall ended any such plans. In three months Southern's earnings fell 35 percent. On top of this, the company had to endure regulations imposed by state and federal agencies who, with many citizens, felt the railroads had grown too powerful. For example, the North Carolina legislature imposed maximum intrastate passengers fares, with fines and imprisonment for ticket agents who ignored the ruling.

In the face of recession and regulation, Southern began laying off workers to cut costs. Almost 600 men were laid off at Spencer early in 1908, 400 of them on March 10. Spencer's first newspaper, the *Crescent*, lamented that "for many weeks our citizens have looked gloomily at the great yard and shops across Salisbury Avenue and

wondered sadly when the stir of old time activity would again gladden their hearts and ensure relief from want." The community was "plunged in gloom" because many laid-off employees had left the area. In late May the railway obtained loans to avoid bankruptcy, and the economy mercifully improved during the summer.

By 1910 Southern's fortunes had recovered, and it implemented long-delayed plans for improving Spencer Shops. The company had wanted to build a new storehouse/office complex beside the back shop since 1905. The building, begun in 1910 and completed in 1911, was similar to the original storehouse/office building but larger and more substantial due to brick construction. A two-story office complex filled a quarter of the building. The shops' master mechanic had his office here and was surrounded by pay clerks, telephone operators, and administrative assistants. While most of the building was storage space, it was called the "master mechanic's office" by workers and still carries that unofficial title.

From a window in the storehouse section shop workers picked up safety equipment such as gloves, steel-toed boots, and protective eyewear. Clerks watched stockpiles of tools and parts of all shapes and sizes. Each month foremen in various departments at the shops requisitioned supplies from the

storehouse. To control costs and reduce waste, storehouse clerks sometimes gave a foreman less of an item than he had ordered, which brought many an irate foreman to the storehouse. Clerks also kept busy filling orders from other shops and terminals as the Spencer storehouse became the main supply distribution center for Southern's eastern lines. Supply trains left the storehouse daily, and a special train delivered such things as toilet articles, brooms, oil, and lamps to track maintenance crews who lived along the tracks in converted cars for days at a time. Though it seems mundane, the work of storehouse staff was essential to proper functioning of the shops.

In 1904 a railroad writer hailing construction of the back shop noted that boiler repair operations at Spencer were small because the "excellent water" used in locomotives there resulted in fewer boiler breakdowns. Excellent water or not, the railroad eventually decided that the boilermakers, who had shared a building with painters and cab repairmen, should have a larger, better-equipped building of their own. To do this the company produced yet another series of building and department changes. In 1911 workers dismantled the building the blacksmiths had originally shared with boilermakers and constructed in its place a sturdy 80-by-150-foot brick boiler shop. The blacksmiths moved into the original

North Carolina Division of Archives and History
Transfer shed workers sorted and moved freight between cars bound for different destinations.

Scores of machines to make and repair locomotive parts rest in the back shop under the balcony in September 1949.

machine shop building which since 1905 had been shared by boilermakers, painters, and cab repairers. Separate and smaller buildings were built north of the back shop as cab and paint shops.

The new boiler shop contained tools to cut, bend, roll, or pound metal into any size and shape. These included bending rolls (which rolled flat metal into cylinders to be used as boiler sections or courses), flange presses for flattening metal to a desired thickness, and multiple-spindle drills for drilling holes in flue and firebox sheets. Smaller metal-working equipment included punches, shears, electric cutting and grinding machines, rivet heaters, staybolt threading and cutting machines, and oxy-acetylene cutting and welding devices.

Southern wasted little time in improving the Spencer terminal facilities as well. In 1913 the line had the

enormous but outdated coaling trestle torn down and built a modern 110-foot-high coal chute near the same area. Included was a fenced-off storage field said to hold 200,000 tons of coal. A motorized belt of buckets lifted coal from there to the chute and dumped it into an electric tipple which poured the coal into locomotive tenders parked on the four tracks which ran through or beside the chute. About 100 engines per day passed through the coaling station, which could load over 500 tons of coal in 24 hours. Because of the chute's automation, only two or three men per shift were required to operate it. Coal chute workers also filled locomotive tenders with water and sand boxes with sand from pipes which swung out from the chute over the locomotive.

At this time the railroad also built a new high-capacity sand house several yards west of the old one. In the new building sand to be dried fell through a cylindrical dome which revolved around a heated core. Compressed air blew the dried sand through pipes to the coal chute.

Another component of the 1913 expansion was a new oil house. The first "oil house" had been little more than a shack where oil drums were stored, but the new oil house (a rather plain 63-by-43-foot building) contained five storage tanks with a total capacity of nearly 50,000 gallons. The oil was used for lubrication in shop machines, locomotives, and rail car axle bearings. An elaborate piping system delivered the oil to shop buildings.

Many shop workers expected (and hoped) that a new roundhouse would be part of the expansion. Shopmen in the old roundhouse had complained about its small size for years. In 1908 the *Spencer Crescent* reported that

INTERIOR ELECTRIC POWER HOUSE. SOUTHERN R. R. SHOPS, Spencer, N. C.

North Carolina Division of Archives and History

Needs for electricity in the back shop required expansion of the power house, which contained the latest power-generating equipment.

many new Southern locomotives stuck out of the short stalls in the roundhouse and that in maintaining them workers were exposed to the elements, causing many cases of colds and flu.

The shopmen were relieved when, in 1911, Southern began building a new 90-foot turntable southwest of the old roundhouse. Newspapers boasted that a tremendous 40-stall roundhouse would be built there. The new turntable began operating in 1912, but more financial uncertainty at Southern and the onset of World War I delayed construction of the roundhouse. In fact, no roundhouse was ever built at the spot, and it would be 12 years before a new roundhouse finally replaced the original.

Improvements at Spencer between 1911 and 1913 helped make the busy shops even busier. In 1913 828 locomotives were serviced or repaired at the shops. All repairs were classified on one of five levels with class one being a complete overhaul and class five being light maintenance in the roundhouse. Twelve locomotives received class one repairs, and 74 received extensive class two repairs, mostly in the back shop. The 288 class three, 276 class four, and 180 class five

repairs performed in the roundhouse covered tasks such as changing wheels, adjusting siderods, and replacing springs and binders.

Most of the repairs were made to the 340 locomotives based at Spencer which rolled over a large portion of the Southern system. The railway was divided into geographic units called divisions. The number and size of divisions shifted frequently, but in the early 1900s there were 15 divisions consisting of between 130 and 795 miles of track. Locomotives serviced at Spencer operated in six divisions containing most Southern trackage between Greenville, South Carolina, and Washington east of the Appalachians.

Except in the economic crisis of 1907, freight carried over these divisions increased steadily, requiring the addition of larger and stronger freight cars. After 1910 Southern increasingly relied on steel boxcars instead of weaker wooden ones. The new steel cars and an increasing number of cars to be repaired prompted Southern to expand the Spencer car repair facilities in 1916. The company once again called on the Pettyjohn Company to dismantle the old car repair shed and construct a new one on the same spot.

Workers got an idea how big the new building would be when the original office/storehouse complex, nearly 100 yards south of the old repair shed, was moved to the other side of the back shop to make room for the construction.

Finished in September 1917, the new car repair shed was three stories high, 110 feet wide, and 600 feet long, comparable in size to the back shop. Several tracks passed through the building, which was open at both ends. It also had a 50-foot-by-105-foot wing to house machinery. Equipment included traveling electric cranes and machines to cut and shape sheets of steel. Some of the new machines required alternating electric current, but the shops' powerhouse only supplied direct current. So on September 1, 1917, the shops began receiving 400 kilowatts of alternating current from a local utility, the first purchased electricity. Dependence on external electricity gradually increased as more machines requiring alternating current were added.

Within a few years, 200 cars per day received repairs at the new shed, which had over 300 employees. The carmen possessed skills and knowledge to make any repair to both wooden and metal passenger and freight cars. They worked most frequently with wheels, axles, and brake systems but could also shorten or lengthen cars, make them stronger by adding metal support beams, and even change their basic structure.

Inspectors in the freight yard tested brakes, journal bearings, and coupling units on cars arriving from across the Southern system. In a practice known as "pooling," Southern also allowed freight cars from other companies into its trains. This prevented transfer of cargo as cars moved from the territory of one company to that of another. Any car needing repair, regardless of its parent company, was labeled a "bad order" car and shoved by a switcher to a special track which led into the car sheds. Another switch engine then pushed a whole string of cars into the building at once. The

David Driscoll/SRHA collection

This April 1940 view shows the landscaped park outside the master mechanic's office near Salisbury Avenue and the picket fence lining the property.

David Driscoll/SRHA collection

With a full load of coal and steam appearing at the cylinder cocks to emit condensed water, engine No. 4832 heads out on a run, passing the 1913 sand house on Aug. 24, 1947.

North Carolina Division of Archives and History

The giant coal chute, built in 1913, could load about 100 engines a day with over 500 tons of coal.

carmen started with the first one and proceeded down the line repairing problems noted by inspectors. When they had finished the last car, a switch engine pushed the string of repaired cars out of the building and pushed more "bad order" cars in. In later years the carmen used motorized winches to pull cars into the shed.

If repairs were made to a car from another railroad, that company eventually paid Southern for the work. Inspectors from the Association of American Railroads, an organization representing the nation's major rail companies, frequently showed up at Spencer and other large shops to ensure that all cars received equal treatment. Spencer carmen grew uneasy when AAR inspectors arrived because even the suggestion of improper care of another company's car might result in severe reprimand or dismissal. Many inspectors differed with the carmen as to the manner in which repairs were to be carried out, and accusations of improper repairs

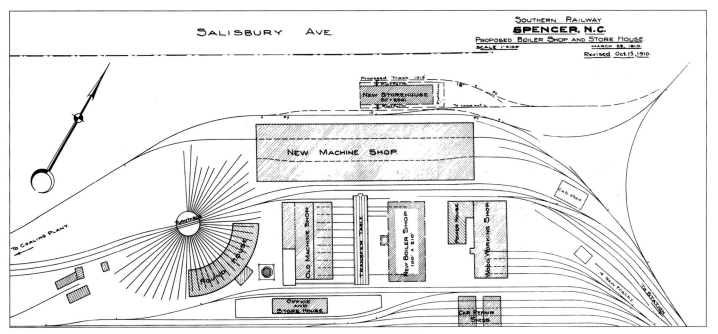

SALISBURY AVE.

SOUTHERN RAILWAY
SPENCER, N.C.
PROPOSED BOILER SHOP AND STORE HOUSE
SCALE 1"=100'
MARCH 29, 1910.
Revised Oct. 15, 1910.

North Carolina Division of Archives and History

In 1910 the back shop, then called the "machine shop," dominated the Shops. Also shown was the new storehouse and master mechanic's office.

might stem more from matters of procedure than actual negligence. Foremen at Spencer were aware of this, and carmen who lost jobs at the request of AAR inspectors often were re-hired after the inspector had left.

From the completion of the back shop in 1905 to the opening of the car shed in 1917 the capacity of the shops more than tripled. The number of employees nearly doubled to over 1300. The roundhouse, terminal facilities, and freight yard buzzed with activity 24 hours a day, and other buildings operated on two eight-hour shifts. Thick smoke from hundreds of puffing locomotives and the power house's huge smokestacks constantly bathed the shop buildings and drifted over the town of Spencer. In the evenings the smoke combined with the steady hum of machines and the shops' powerful electric lights to produce an eerie scene. Underneath the smoke, noise, and lights, the constant movement of men, rail cars, and locomotives caused the shops and freight yard to resemble an ant colony busy at work.

David Driscoll/SRHA collection

The back of the master mechanic's office was the storehouse, home to small locomotive parts. This scene shows a spotless room on Sept. 29, 1946.

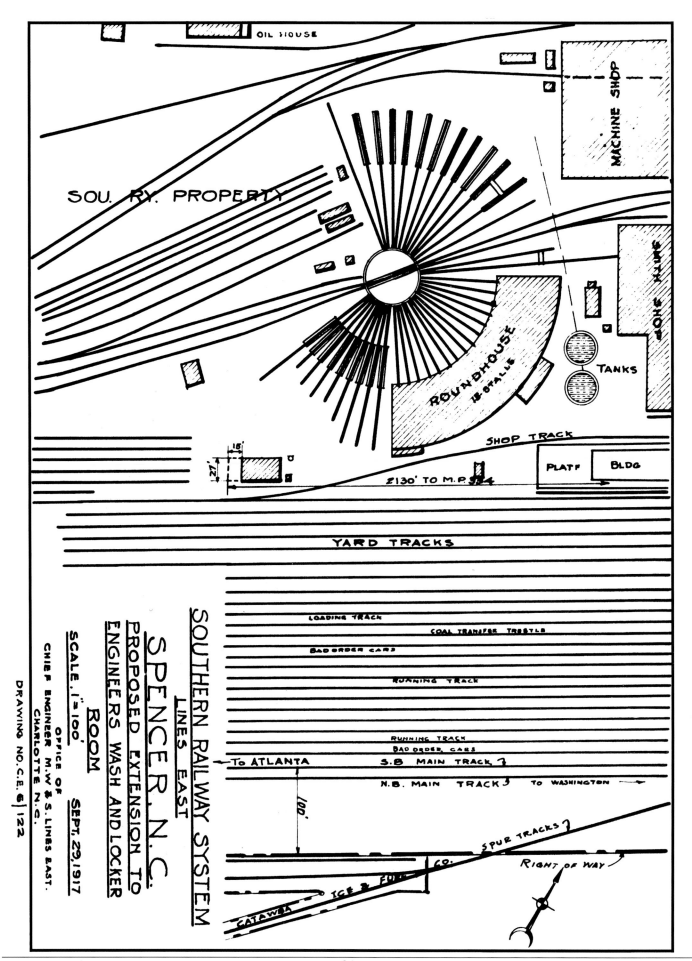

OIL HOUSE

MACHINE SHOP

SOU. RY. PROPERTY

SMITH SHOP

ROUNDHOUSE 16 STALLS

Tanks

SHOP TRACK

2130' TO M.P. 354

PLATF   BLDG

YARD TRACKS

LOADING TRACK

COAL TRANSFER TRESTLE

BAD ORDER CARS

RUNNING TRACK

RUNNING TRACK

BAD ORDER CARS

To ATLANTA   S.B. MAIN TRACK

N.B. MAIN TRACK   TO WASHINGTON

100'

SPUR TRACKS

RIGHT OF WAY

CATAWBA   ICE & FUEL CO.

SOUTHERN RAILWAY SYSTEM
LINES EAST

SPENCER, N.C.

PROPOSED EXTENSION TO
ENGINEERS WASH AND LOCKER
ROOM

SCALE, 1"=100'   SEPT. 29, 1917

OFFICE OF
CHIEF ENGINEER M.W.& S. LINES EAST.
CHARLOTTE N.C.

DRAWING NO. C.E. 6 122

The Town of Spencer

1900 - 1920

4

Spencer's citizens were not about to let the shops grow without them. Most of the railroad men who settled in the new town were energetic, literate, and highly motivated. Like most railroad workers, their wages were higher than average, and they intended to build an above average town in which to raise their children.

Education was a prime consideration, and a four-room school operated by a Dr. W. L. Newsom had attracted 120 students by 1901. In 1905 the town passed a bond issue for a larger brick school on Carolina Avenue. Critics charged that there would never be enough children in Spencer to fill the building, but only nine years later a tremendous increase in enrollment forced the town to double its size. A high school in the new building consisted of grades eight through eleven; the twelfth grade would not be added until 1944.

On the night of March 1, 1925, the oldest portion of the school caught fire, and 16 tons of coal in its basement created an inferno which Spencerites still remember as the most spectacular fire to hit the downtown area. The fire destroyed the building, but a new and even larger one was soon built. Until the Spencer High School was replaced by the North Rowan High School in 1958, its athletic teams were appropriately known as the Railroaders.

The period 1905 to 1907 saw many developments in Spencer in addition to a new school. Electric street lights were installed on Salisbury Avenue where macadamized paving and a sidewalk replaced dust and mud. Connection to the Salisbury water and sewer systems and a new well and pump station on Sixth Street provided water to houses and businesses being constructed with indoor plumbing. New houses popped

up all the way from downtown Spencer to the Salisbury city limits, making it difficult to determine where one town ended and the other began.

In 1905 entrepreneurs built an electric streetcar line from Salisbury to Spencer which remained extremely popular until 1938 when buses took over the service. Prior to the streetcar line many people commuted between Salisbury and Spencer on the "shop train," which made a round trip three times daily to provide transportation for shop workers. The ride took only a few minutes, but some workers enjoyed an ongoing card game that picked up everyday at the same place it had stopped the day before. The shop train left from the original master mechanic's office/store house, and townspeople went onto shop grounds to board it, a privilege later denied them.

Not all early town projects were on the scale of the school and streetcar line. The first jail, built on Fourth Street in 1901, was seven by eight feet and held only one prisoner. It was built of heavy lumber with iron bars on its windows, but lacked one important element--a floor. To escape, one merely tilted the little jail over. This was done so many times that the jail was on its side as often as it was upright. Many inmates were very drunk, however, and this obvious escape route often eluded them. Soon the town built a more secure jail, and the old one became a wood shed.

The town never outgrew its connection to the railroad which had created it. By 1905 it was clear that the small YMCA was woefully inadequate. Several boarding houses operated in Spencer and East Spencer but could not accommodate all the trainmen forced to "sleep over" between runs. According to federal law, trainmen coming into Spencer after a 16-hour run had to wait eight hours

before beginning another, hours often used for sleep. Southern decided to help with a new YMCA. The company's chief architect, Frank P. Milburn, who later designed a large passenger depot for Salisbury, designed a new YMCA building costing $20,000. Town and YMCA officials bought a plot at the corner of Sixth Street and Salisbury Avenue, which brought the total cost to $27,000. Southern graciously contributed $15,000 to the project. The YMCA raised the remaining $12,000 through subscriptions sold to town folk and railroad employees in a vigorous publicity campaign.

The building, opened with much fanfare on March 23, 1907, was more wonderful than the people had dared imagine. It had 48 bedrooms, bathrooms with showers and tubs (plumbing installed), reading rooms, a library, restaurant, bowling alley, and barber shop. By 1912 the YMCA had 555 members, about half of whom were non-resident trainmen who used the Y when they had a layover in Spencer. The "Christian" in Young Men's Christian Association was expressed in Sunday worship services and weekly Bible study. The Y also became a community center as private organizations and the town government rented space for meetings. Townspeople attended lectures on religious and political topics, and the restaurant became a favorite meeting place for citizens and shop workers. Southern Railway's continued sponsorship of the YMCA was yet another reminder of the close relationship between company and town.

The Spencer YMCA became the center of a vibrant downtown which by 1910 included two banks, two office buildings, five general merchandise stores, two drugstores, and many other businesses. The 1910 census revealed 1,915 people in Spencer, the

SOUTHERN RAILWAY Y. M. C. A. BUILDING, Spencer, N. C.

North Carolina Division of Archives and History

The spacious new Spencer YMCA opened in 1907; citizens and Southern Railway cooperated to fund the project. At right: one of the tokens from the YMCA.

population having tripled since 1900 in direct proportion to the increasing capacity of the shops.

But amidst this phenomenal growth and prosperity tragedy sometimes touched the people of Spencer. Train wrecks, the most feared events in the town, took the lives of many trainmen who lived there. Several wrecks affecting Spencer also drew regional or national attention. The first, in 1901, involved a train carrying the Buffalo Bill Wild West Show. The show, famous throughout the United States and Europe, boasted over 1,200 participants including the incredible sharpshooter, Annie Oakley. Buffalo Bill and his entourage played at

Charlotte on October 29 and boarded the show's three trains for a night trip to Danville, Virginia.

At the time, the Southern main line was single-tracked, and a few miles north of Spencer dispatchers ordered a southbound freight to a siding to allow the northbound show trains to pass. The freight engineer assumed the show had only one train, and after the first passed he eased back on to the main line. Within a few minutes he saw the headlight of the second show train. Both locomotive crews jumped in the nick of time, but the sleeping animals and people on the show train had no chance to escape before the head-on collision.

No people were killed, but several were severely injured, Annie Oakley among them. Doctors said she would never shoot, or even walk, again. Two years and five operations later she was back in the show, however, as accurate a shot as ever. Local legend maintained that the 41-year-old Oakley's brown hair turned white within hours after the crash. Years later, Oakley substantiated the story.

Buffalo Bill's horses did not fare as well, for 110 of them were killed or injured severely and destroyed after the wreck. Other animals escaped, and residents of Spencer woke the next morning to find strange new animals in their fields.

The freight engineer ran from the scene and was never heard from again. The conductor resigned on the spot. Locals claimed that Buffalo Bill acquired a tremendous shotgun that he used in his shows and went searching for the crew of the freight train. If true, it is easy to see why the engineer fled.

Another wreck affecting Spencer involved a mail train with the number 97 which became a household name. In 1902 Southern won a contract with the U.S. Post Office to carry mail between Washington and New Orleans. The Post Office paid $140,000 annually, but the railroad had to refund a portion of the fee if the mail trains ran late. On September 27, 1903, mail train No. 97 left Washington after considerable delays. When it arrived at its first crew-change point, Monroe, Virginia, it was already an hour behind schedule. The train consisted of two railway post office cars, where clerks sorted mail en route, an express car, and a baggage car. At its head was locomotive 1102, a fast 4-6-0 model.

Conductor John T. Blair, a Spencer native, boarded the train at Monroe. Thomas H. Kritzer, also of Spencer and one of the most respected engineers on the line, was also supposed to board at Monroe. A scheduling error delayed him, and Joseph A. "Steve" Broady, an experienced engineer new to the railway, was forced to

North Carolina Division of Archives and History

In 1905 streetcars began running between Salisbury and Spencer. This photo was taken in Salisbury.

take over. Broady was determined to make up some of the lost time as he headed to Spencer, the next crew-change point. Witnesses reported that No. 97 was making fantastic speeds as it neared Danville. Just north of Danville, at the end of a three-mile descending grade, was the curved Stillhouse Trestle, one of the most dangerous spots on the main line. Broady, who apparently ignored signs to decrease speed, realized too late that he was going too fast to make the curve. A long, piercing blast of the locomotive's whistle, perhaps a warning to the brakeman to apply the handbrakes, alerted nearby residents that something was wrong. As the train approached the trestle, it derailed and plunged into the ravine beneath it. All crewmen were killed along with five postal clerks, 11 men in all. Six more clerks were severely injured, but one man, a station clerk who had been mistakenly left on the train as it sped out of Monroe, miraculously escaped unharmed.

Crews from Spencer Shops raced north to retrieve the locomotive from the ravine. One shopman recalled that the locomotive arrived in Spencer "literally wrapped up in red mud. The jacket was torn loose and some of the other parts were broken or bent. It had taken two derricks to hoist it from the river bank up to the track...." Despite the damage, the Spencer shopmen quickly rebuilt number 1102. It worked for Southern until the late 1930s when it lost its final battle—to a scrapyard torch.

After a period of mourning for Blair, the Spencer conductor killed in the wreck, most of the town seemed to have forgotten about it. Disasters were common on America's railroads, and the wreck of a mail train in which "only" 11 people were killed was not special. Soon, however, David Graves George of Franklin Junction, Virginia, penned a poem about the wreck which he began singing to the music of "The Ship That Never Returned," an old nineteenth-century ballad. Versions of the song, usually titled "Wreck of the Ol' 97," could be heard on back porches and in minstrel shows across the South. In 1924 Vernon Dahlhart, a star in the infant radio industry, began singing the song on the air. It became a national hit, and many people claimed authorship before a court ruled in George's favor.

FIRST NATIONAL BANK AND FIFTH AVENUE, Spencer, N. C.

North Carolina Division of Archives and History
The First National Bank symbolized the economic good fortune of prosperous Spencer.

For Spencer the ballad had special meaning. In one line engineer Broady (or "Brady" in the ballad) is told to "put 'er in Spencer on time," or make up the lost time at any cost. The ballad stretches the truth, but Spencer natives visiting other parts of the country describe their hometown simply by citing it.

Another wreck, three years after Old 97's, involved the man after whom the town and shops had been named. By 1906 Samuel Spencer was one of the most respected men in the rail industry. In 1904 he spearheaded an effort against the Esch-Townsend bill, a congressional measure allowing the Interstate Commerce Commission to set freight rates, something most railroad presidents believed would ruin the industry. Spencer, one of the first railroad men to emphasize public relations, criss-crossed the country speaking to citizens' groups, newspaper editors, and congressmen. The Esch-Townsend bill was defeated in the Senate largely because of his efforts.

On Thanksgiving Day, 1906, at the height of his popularity and career, Sam Spencer began a much needed vacation. With friends and business associates he left Washington for Greensboro and several days of bird hunting. Spencer's private car was at the end of a passenger train, No. 33, which was an hour behind schedule because of mechanical problems. With the delay the train was only a few minutes ahead of another southbound passenger train, No. 37. A few miles north of the station at Lawyers, Virginia, at about 6:15 a.m., No. 33 came to a dead stop. Newspaper accounts said the train halted for a minor repair. Following standard procedure for an emergency stop, the flagman of No. 33 began walking back to warn any other approaching trains, apparently unaware that there was another train so close behind. Before he could give a proper signal, No. 37 came roaring around a bend. An operator at a block station had allowed the second train to proceed without receiving word that the track ahead was clear. Newspapers claimed the operator fled his post after the accident and vanished.

Number 37 barreled past the flagman and hit Spencer's stopped private car at about 30 miles an hour. Gas tanks underneath the car exploded and the resulting fire spread to other cars, but their passengers were rescued. Seven passengers in Spencer's car were killed instantly: Spencer, three friends, a dispatcher, and two porters. Spencer's secretary and another porter somehow survived.

During World War I and for three decades thereafter Spencer Shops was a heavy industry site at its peak. In this 1947 view 0-6-0-locomotive No. 1742 is in switching service at the Spencer yard.

The engineers on both trains were good friends from Spencer. They were elated to find that each had survived the accident, but their elation turned to sorrow when they learned that the president of the company had died. Shocked citizens of Spencer held a memorial service in the YMCA and sent a large delegation to the funeral the next day in Washington. Sam Spencer was very popular among employees. After his death thousands of them volunteered to have a small amount deducted from their pay each month to fund a monument to him. The bronze statue, designed by noted American sculptor Daniel Chester French, was dedicated at the Southern station in Atlanta on May 21, 1910.

Following Spencer's death, vice president A. B. Andrews was asked to succeed his good friend as president. He refused, citing too much time away from his family and friends. His son remained trustee for railway property in Spencer until 1908 when the Georgia Industrial Realty Company, a Southern subsidiary, took over the deeds. William W. Finley of Mississippi eventually became president. Finley was talented and well-liked by employees, but no one could ever quite fill the shoes of the man who had built a successful company from the ruins of so many others and given his name to a new railroad town in the Carolina Piedmont.

By 1914 the people of Spencer had weathered the terrible depression of 1908 and had seen friends and neighbors and the president of the railroad killed in accidents, but they had also seen the output of the shops and the population of the town more than double. Southern was pulling in large profits, and rumors circulated that more buildings would be added to the shops complex. Spencer shopmen had reason to believe that good things lay ahead. They could not know that a pivotal event of the twentieth century was about to take place. In late June 1914 shop workers reading newspapers on their breaks learned that the heir to the throne of Austria had been assassinated in a far-

Spencer's railroad cranes cleared wrecks for many years. Here a crew poses in front of one of the giant cranes based at Spencer Shops.

North Carolina Division of Archives and History

A crane crew stands before a Pacific-type locomotive salvaged from a wreck site. African American cooks accompanied crews to provide food on trips which might require several days to recover a wreck.

away Balkan town named Sarajevo. They probably thought little about it, but the murder unleashed incredible destructive tensions which had been building for years among leading nations of Europe. World War I began in August, and Americans watched to see how they would be affected.

The war eventually caused rail traffic along the East Coast to increase as the warring nations began buying munitions and supplies in the United States. After President Woodrow Wilson announced America's entry into the war in April 1917, rail traffic virtually exploded, and it became clear that the nation's railroads were not up to the task. Trains loaded with war materials backed up for miles trying to get to crowded Atlantic ports, causing a critical boxcar shortage.

In December President Wilson created the United States Railroad Administration (USRA) and put railroads under the USRA where they remained until February 1920. The railroads operated with somewhat more efficiency under the USRA, but it required tremendous effort on the part of the entire industry. The Spencer Shops faced problems similar to those at shops and terminals across the nation. They had to meet an increased demand with fewer workers as many shop employees and trainmen entered the armed forces.

Foremen, master mechanics, and even high ranking officials toiled on the shop floor to keep the trains rolling. In many towns women took vacant railroad jobs.

The people of Spencer rejoiced when the war ended in November 1918, but they had to endure one more war-related test. Before the armistice was signed an influenza epidemic, dubbed the "Spanish Flu," began to spread across Europe like fire through dry leaves. The dispersion of the multi-national Allied forces at the war's end helped spread the disease, and American military personnel carried it across the Atlantic to their hometowns. Flu soon appeared in Greenville, South Carolina, where recruits from Rowan County were training. In October the flu arrived in Landis, in southern Rowan County, and in Salisbury and Spencer soon thereafter. It reached epidemic proportions overnight and peaked on October 19 when more than 1,000 cases were reported in the area. The county's public health officer closed all schools, theaters, and churches. The town of Spencer set a $50 fine for holding meetings of any kind.

The epidemic was costly for Rowan County industry. Not only were workers succumbing to the disease, but many who were healthy refused to leave home for fear of infection. Several textile mills shut down. The Spencer Shops were hard

hit but remained open with a skeleton work force. George L. Burke, a shop worker, later remembered that people were "dying like flies" and those who ventured out walked around with rags over their faces. He recalled that coffins at the Spencer depot piled up to the building's windows. Burke caught the flu himself and almost died. He lost 30 days from work and claimed that they were the only sick days he took in 50 years.

The epidemic subsided by November but left many dead and severely curtailed shop activities for several weeks. In a few months the flu claimed over 500,000 lives in the United States and up to ten million lives worldwide.

While the flu raged through Spencer, and for several months thereafter, the nation's railroads remained under the control of the USRA. Company owners loathed continued government control of their property, but employees were not entirely displeased. They had been granted several concessions by the USRA which included a 52 percent wage increase to counter wartime inflation, an eight-hour workday, and greater bargaining power for labor unions. The federal government ended its control of the railroads in 1920 and set up an agency to oversee labor issues in the industry.

Roundhouse foreman Bob Julian with diesel No. 4114, Sept. 29, 1946. Julian went to work for Southern in 1897—the year after Spencer Shops was founded. The roundhouse at Spencer was named after Bob Julien.

Expansion of Southern Railway, Spencer Shops, and the Town of Spencer

5

After federal control ended in 1920, Southern Railway faced challenges posed by powerful labor unions and a rapidly growing trucking industry which threatened railroad revenues. Nonetheless, a growing economy allowed Southern's revenues to outstrip expenses. Fairfax Harrison, who became company president in 1913, pumped earnings into physical improvements and improved service. A new passenger train, the *Crescent Limited*, began a regular New York-to-New Orleans run in 1925. To pull the Limited and help smooth out mountainous routes, Harrison ordered more 4-6-2 Pacific locomotives in 1923. The new Pacifics were built to specifications set by Southern engineers and painted "Virginia" green and silver with gold lettering, a color scheme which would become recognized nationally.

Many colorful Pacifics were based at Spencer, giving further impetus for enlarged terminal facilities. Southern's only other attempt at a new round-

house for Spencer had stalled after completion of a turntable in 1912, but this time the company was committed to building a roundhouse worthy of the exceptional locomotives which would be serviced there.

After careful investigation Southern officials decided the 90-foot turntable of 1912 was outdated and abandoned plans to build a roundhouse around it. In February 1924 the company announced it would tear down the 15-stall roundhouse built in 1896 and construct a massive 37-stall concrete monolith in its place.

Engineers and workmen worked hurriedly: every day of construction was a day the shops were crippled for lack of a true roundhouse. Workmen dismantled the walls and frame of the old roundhouse but simply covered over much of the foundation and piping with dirt and cinders and poured a concrete floor for the new building. When the 37-stall roundhouse was renovated in 1995 as a museum, surprised workmen uncovered the buried

foundation of the original roundhouse, nearly a century after it had been laid.

The new roundhouse was put into service on December 2, 1924, only ten months after construction was announced. The building's steel frame supported heavy brick and concrete walls. The steel slab roof had a top layer of tar and gravel and was pierced by smoke jacks over the stalls. Each stall had a depth of 106 feet to accommodate almost any locomotive in Southern's vast fleet.

The stalls of the new roundhouse were numbered consecutively from left to right and generally divided according to purpose. The first two stalls were for repairs requiring more than one day but not important enough for the back shop. Stalls three through eight were equipped with pits for dropping driving wheels; nine through eleven had pits for dropping truck and tender wheels. Wheel sets could be rolled from the building via three doors in the back wall. Stalls 12

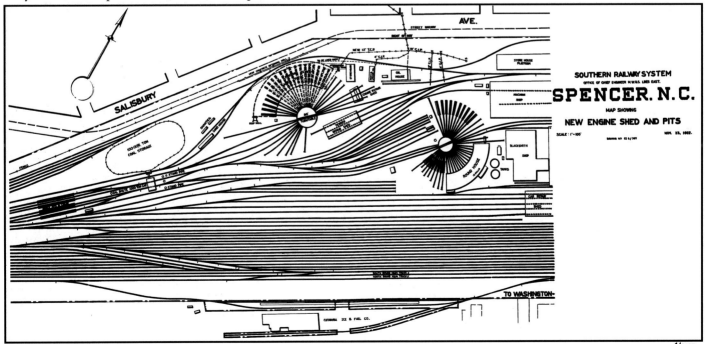

North Carolina Division of Archives and History

In the early 1920s Spencer Shops had two turntables but still lacked a large, modern roundhouse.

This view shows the stalls around tracks 5-12 with three water tanks behind the roundhouse.

through 37 were for general repair. Shallow pits ran most of the length of each stall, giving workers access below locomotives.

The general repair stalls were usually labeled by the type of locomotive which could be parked there. Stalls 12 through 15 were for small switch, or yard, engines. Passenger engines occupied the middle stalls, while the stalls on the right side were for freight engines. The exact points of the divisions are uncertain, and exceptions were the rule. If an engine needed quick repairs, it was put into any available stall.

A machine shop on the back of the roundhouse contained 11 electrically powered machines which enabled shopmen to make minor alterations to locomotive parts. The floors of the machine shop, roundhouse stalls, and back shop were made of creosoted wood blocks covering a cement base. A smaller room on the back of the roundhouse housed an office where employees picked up work orders for locomotives.

A small brick building behind the right side of the roundhouse contained equipment for recycling water extracted from locomotive boilers.

Once filtered, the water was used to wash and refill boilers in repaired locomotives ready to be "fired up" again. Live steam from the power plant could be piped into boilers to aid in building steam. Locomotives needing minor repairs might be in the roundhouse only a few hours, so their boilers were still hot when re-filled. Recycled hot water was used to fill these boilers as cold water might have buckled or cracked the metal. Hot water also was pumped to a cleaning station by the right side of the roundhouse. At this "wash track" workmen used high pressure hoses to clean locomotive exteriors with an 180-degree mixture of water and solvents.

Providing heat for the 120,000-square-foot roundhouse was difficult. The stalls had no doors, and rain and bitter cold penetrated the work area. Steam from the power plant produced some heat, but the primary heat source was simple and inadequate pot-bellied stoves.

While the primitive stoves proved incapable, much equipment at the new roundhouse was the most advanced available. Turret lathes with individual electric motors crowded the machine shop. Pneumatic wrenches,

boring mills, and other portable machine tools lined the walls. Overhead cranes, for transporting parts, moved the entire length of the roundhouse on rails 29 feet apart and more than 20 feet off the ground. A ten-ton crane served stalls one through eight where wheel sets were removed, and at least one 1 1/2-ton crane operated in stalls nine through thirty-seven. The 100-foot turntable for the roundhouse was the largest ever built at Spencer and accommodated almost every locomotive on the Southern roster. The turntable rotated inside a concrete pit with a 101-foot diameter and was powered by two 25-horsepower alternating-current electric motors.

The estimated final cost of the roundhouse was $500,000 (about $4.7 million in 1996 dollars). It was christened the Bob Julian Roundhouse after Spencer's hard working, irascible roundhouse supervisor, the only roundhouse in the system named for a person. For decades the Julian Roundhouse was one of the finest on the railway and a source of pride for Spencer workers.

The roundhouse wasn't the only major construction project of 1924.

North Carolina Division of Archives and History

2-8-2 locomotive No. 4835 sits near the wash tracks at the Bob Julian Roundhouse.

Just northwest of the building Southern built a new shop to repair locomotive flues, formerly done in the back shop. Flues were long, narrow steel tubes inside boilers which carried fire, soot, and hot gasses from the firebox through the water to the smokebox. As many as 100 flues inside a boiler helped create draft for the fire, and heat passing through them created more steam from the surrounding water. The intense heat caused the ends of the flues to wear quickly. The Federal Railroad Administration (the government's watchdog agency for railroads) required railroads to remove and repair flues periodically to reduce accidents from broken or leaking flues and let inspectors examine the interiors of boilers.

The flue shop (51 feet 10 inches by 155 feet 8 inches) was completed a few weeks after the roundhouse and contained torches for cutting off burned flue ends, electric welders for applying new ends, and machines to roll completely new flues from flat strips of steel. Almost one-third of the new building contained a shop where craftsmen worked with tin or babbitt, a soft metal alloy used in axle bearings. The construction of the roundhouse and flue shop was the last major expansion at Spencer and dramatical-

ly increased the capacity of the shops.

Like most of the nation's larger railroads, Southern prospered into the late 1920s. Officials poured profits into new tracks, stations, and shop buildings. The company also invested in what would be its last batch of new steam locomotives in 1928. The 37 stalls at Spencer's Julian Roundhouse quickly filled with the snorting giants. Most rested there only a few hours before being sent back into service. Twenty-four hours a day the Spencer Shops and yard were a flurry of activity reflective of the good times enjoyed by the railroad industry.

The Great Depression and World War II

To Southern it seemed the good times would never end. The collapse of the stock market in October 1929 surprised the line as it did most of the nation. In the downward economic spiral which followed, banks failed and factory orders fell precipitously, resulting in large layoffs. Within three years 25 percent of American workers were unemployed. Railroad revenues fell almost 50 percent from $4.9 billion in 1929 to $2.5 billion in 1932. In 1931 Southern operated at a loss for the first time. President Harrison

began a vigorous cost-cutting program and shut down small branch lines, stations, and shops. As minor shops closed, repair activity was consolidated at Spencer, the major shop complex on Southern's eastern lines.

There was more work to be done at Spencer than when the economy had been healthy. Besides work from closed shops, the men at Spencer struggled to keep Southern's aging locomotives in operation. Buying new locomotives was out of the question. By 1932 Spencer Shops serviced 75 engines daily with one complete overhaul turned out of the back shop each weekday.

The increased workload didn't mean more jobs. In fact, there were occasional layoffs. Trains arriving at Spencer often carried several men looking for work, any work. They seldom found it. "We didn't look on them as bums," a retiree remembers. "They were people down on their luck because of something that had hit everyone." Families near the tracks became accustomed to men knocking on their doors for a bite to eat.

Activity at the shops meant that mass unemployment did not plague Spencer, but the financial crisis did not leave the community unscathed. Spencer's only bank remained solvent

David Driscoll captured these passeger, freight and yard locomotives or goat, on film outside the roundhouse in September 1947.

until 1932 but then closed, much to the chagrin of depositors. Spencer officials would not lure another bank to the town until 1943. Business activity slowed considerably. A Spencer native remembers that he and other children played freely in the streets because few cars disturbed them. Parts of Spencer seemed to him more a ghost town than an industrial center. Smokers unable to afford factory cigarettes made do with nickel bags of tobacco shavings which one rolled by hand in cigarette paper. The townfolk, mostly Democrats, chided Republican president Herbert Hoover by dubbing the tobacco "Hoover dust."

Despite the terrible economic situation, some hearty individuals launched businesses in Spencer in the 1930s. In 1932 Gordon Brandt opened a supermarket, reportedly the state's first, on Fifth Street. The new concept was slow to catch on, and the store closed in 1936. Brandt went to California to observe techniques for keeping vegetables fresh. Returning in 1937, he introduced Brandt's Open Air Market, which remained open until 1946. In 1929 C. E. Kneeburg opened a watch repair school on Salisbury Avenue near the shops. To maintain train schedules, watches of railroad men had to function perfectly, and there was a great demand in Spencer for skilled watch repairers. Kneeburg and four other instructors trained mostly disabled persons and

army veterans. The school operated until 1968 and counted over 1,300 graduates.

When World War II began in Europe in 1939, the people of Spencer, like many other Americans, kept their attention on the economy and hoped President Franklin Roosevelt's New Deal would end hard times. On December 7, 1941, however, the Japanese launched a surprise attack against the U.S. naval base at Pearl Harbor in Hawaii, killing over 2,000 Americans. The tragedy launched America into the war, but the nation's railroads resisted another government takeover like that of World War I. This seemed an impossible task as larger armies, a two-front war, and extended American involvement ensured even greater demands on the railroads than in the first war. Rubber rationing meant fewer tires, which severely curtailed the trucking industry, while enemy submarines reduced coastal shipping, thereby creating even more work for railroads. They responded heroically and avoided federal takeover for the entire war.

The primary reason for the railroads' achievement was that the capacity of rail cars and the power of locomotives had increased dramatically since World War I. Immense steam engines and new freight diesels appeared early in the war. Southern used high-capacity cars purchased before and during the Depression to great advantage. In December 1941

the company moved an entire army division, some 12,000 men, from the East Coast to the West Coast in three days, using 1,543 cars in the process. During the war Southern handled almost 70 percent more traffic than in World War I.

As the global struggle continued, the railroad increased the Spencer work force to between 3,000 and 3,500, the highest in the history of the shops. Though 7,600 Southern employees served in the armed forces, many skilled shopmen were given deferments. Such shopmen and trainmen were often more valuable out of the army than in it.

While the shops did not lose a large number of men to the army, the transfer sheds, with mostly unskilled labor, saw many men drafted. This loss and the increased traffic of wartime caused a manpower shortage at the sheds. Southern met the problem with "womanpower." By October 1943 some 42 women, mostly black, worked at the transfer sheds. Hired as an experiment, they proved apt and efficient. The women wore slacks and overalls and reportedly could be mistaken for men save for an "occasional flash of a red blouse or handkerchief." One reporter noted that the women also improved the behavior and language of the men who began "watching out for the fine points of conduct." To be eligible for their strenuous jobs, the women had to be between 21 and 54 years old, able to read and write, of good general health, and weigh more than 130 pounds. Character was also important; they underwent background checks to ascertain if they were "good citizens." Despite this scrutiny and the hard labor, the women spoke positively of the sheds. They made good money and were happy, one said, to be helping the war effort.

The town of Spencer also supported the war effort. The municipal building became the site of the local rationing board. With streetcar service from Salisbury to Spencer abandoned in 1938 for buses, the Spencer aldermen donated the street rails to the national steel drive. The Works Progress Administration, a federal jobs program, removed the rails and also extended Spencer's water and sewer lines and repaired streets. The town allowed the federal government to train defense workers in the Spencer High School. The hard work was rewarded in 1945 when jubilant residents threw an impromptu parade to celebrate the Allied victory.

Life In A Shop Town

For shopmen and trainmen, relationships developed on the job often carried over into private lives. Spencer was a tight-knit community bound by ties of occupation, friendship, and kinship. Once a family settled in Spencer, they were likely to remain for generations. Shopmen were generally static because of the seniority system. If one transferred to another shops site, even within the same company, he generally lost his seniority, which induced shopmen as a group to stay in the same location as long as possible. Any vacancies in skilled positions were filled from within the shop, so that men could hope to advance to higher positions, such as foreman or even master mechanic, so long as they stayed at the same site. Preference in hiring locally also helped keep Spencer families stationary. Young men who began as helpers and apprentices were usually relatives of shops workers. Spencer neighborhoods ultimately contained several

In the midst of the Great Depression Southern sent many of its engines to Spencer for overhaul, including 2-8-2 No. 4612, on right.

generations of railroad men in close proximity to one another.

The term "like a family," often used to describe industrial communities such as cotton mill towns, issues repeatedly and unrehearsed from the lips of Spencerites describing their town. Frances Vail married a railroad man and moved to Spencer as a young woman. "It was a beautiful community to come into," she recalls. "The people were so friendly, so loving." "The people were concerned about other families," adds Melba Hatley, whose husband Bill, a conductor, was away from home for days at a time. Neighbors knew which trainmen were away at a given time and looked after their families. "Everybody did for everybody else; everybody looked out for one another," Frances Vail explains.

For railroad wives churches, civic groups and clubs such as the Spencer Women's Club, founded in 1946, were opportunities for community involvement. Such organizations had many members and received much coverage in local newspapers, due in part to the permanency of shop employees. Families moving frequently had little cause to join them.

The social interaction provided by these organizations helped relieve boredom for some housewives. Their

husbands' relatively high wages meant that railroad wives rarely held permanent full-time jobs. They worked at home, but they could argue that housework in a shop town was no less strenuous than men's work in the shops or freight yard. Whenever they hung out clothes, soot and smoke from the shops might make them dirtier than before they were washed. Soot permeated houses, especially attics, and built up in layers over the years. The soot made cleaning carpets and floors an adventure. Perhaps the only job more difficult was cleaning up children who came home from improvised playgrounds covered in mud, soot, and cinders.

The activities of children in railroad towns such as Spencer were unique. Pranks included pouring oil on the streetcar rails which ran from Salisbury to Spencer. The children's favorite target was a hilly section of track which streetcars had to climb before reaching the center of town. Grumbling streetcar drivers had to stop and put sand on the tracks at this point to get their cars over the oil.

No sooner had they freed themselves then the drivers ran over railroad torpedoes planted by the children. Torpedoes were small box-like devices which exploded loudly when something heavy ran over them.

David Driscoll photo/SRHA collection

Southern's switchers were revered by their crews. Witness local freight engine No. 809 with No. 728 in the roundhouse on Sept. 15, 1946. Astride its visored headlight: a pair of brass candlesticks for show.

Before radio communication between trains, torpedoes were put on tracks by a brakeman whose train had made an emergency stop. If another train approached, it ran over the torpedoes and the explosions told the engineer that a train was stopped ahead. Torpedoes inevitably found their way into the hands of Spencer children who used them for all sorts of mischief, especially on streetcar rails. The children suffered a major disappointment when buses replaced the streetcars. Some boys tied tin cans behind the buses, but the effect was not as gratifying as exploding torpedoes.

Spencer children did not spend all their time in such deviltry. More often, they played in the large park in the center of town, roller skated up and down the streets (after they had been paved), deftly tip-toed along the ledge around the Methodist church building, or sent aloft homemade hydrogen balloons bearing the message, "If found please write to... ."

Children eagerly watched the high school football team, the Railroaders, battle teams from Salisbury and other nearby towns. Older residents claim that Salisbury once defeated Spencer 99-0 and memorialized the feat on the wall of the Spencer bank, a source of contention for many years thereafter. Children also watched the celebrated

Spencer Shops baseball team play teams from across the state.

Both children and adults had heated political discussions. National and state politics dominated the front pages of the *Spencer News* and *Spencer Crescent* while local events—even an accident or large layoff at the shops—were almost always relegated to the back pages. Spencer residents could sit on their porches and chat with close neighbors about prohibition, a war, the New Deal, or whatever was current news. Gossip might also reveal who in town was a closet Republican. Spencer was a Democratic stronghold which during the 1920s endured three consecutive Republican presidents before Franklin D. Roosevelt was elected in 1932. One longtime resident joked that people in Spencer regarded Roosevelt with "only a little less esteem than Jesus" and added that the president's picture adorned the walls of many Spencer homes, right under the picture of the Lord.

Early Spencer residents also seem to have had little toleration for Catholics. Al Smith, a Catholic, created a great fuss in Spencer as Democratic nominee for president in 1928. The people had to choose between religious and political convictions, and many arguments raged. Only scabs (shopmen who did not join fellow workers in strikes) raised the ire of citizens more than Catholics or Republican presidents. One former resident said with only slight hyperbole: "If there was anything the people of Spencer held against a man it was being either a scab, a Catholic, or a Republican. I shudder to think what would have happened if a man had been all three."

While Spencer's residents discussed politics, the shops complex hummed only yards away. Its powerful electric lights mixed with smoke and soot from locomotives and the powerhouse to create an artificial fog which cloaked the town, a constant reminder of the reason for its existence. To most citizens of Spencer their very identity was their occupation. Pride in work-

0-6-0 locomotive No. 1751 stands ready at the roundhouse in April 1951.

ing for the railroad was most clearly shown in the town's noted Labor Day celebrations. Recognition of Labor Day had started by 1903 and featured a parade and races. In 1906 a union representative was the guest, and in 1909 the organizer of the Farmer's Alliance in North Carolina spoke. The greatest celebrations occurred from 1912 to 1916. Each year a large parade began near Salisbury and ended in Spencer's park in front of the shops where up to 20,000 people gathered. Every union had a float in the parade to symbolize its craft. One machinists' float, for example, boasted a working lathe. Trainmen's unions displayed new boxcars, and the painters marched beside a float with a large map of the Southern system. Celebrations ceased during the 1920s but resumed after World War II.

The images of the railway in Labor Day parades recognized the company which gave the people of Spencer their identity as railroaders. But after establishing the community the company exercised little control, giving inhabitants a dual identity as railroaders and citizens of a vibrant, independent town. Like many cotton mill villages dotting the Piedmont, Spencer had been created solely to house workers of an adjacent industrial complex. But unlike them it had freedom to pursue independent economic development. From Spencer's beginning its business and civic leaders strove to break its status as a single-industry town. In 1908 the Retail Merchant's Association boasted in ads of Spencer's "Splendid Citizenship" which was "Progressive, Public Spirited, and Conservative in Politics." They suggested that, among other industries, Spencer needed a "Mattress Factory, Cotton-Seed Oil Mill, and Paper Pulp Mill."

Several entrepreneurs established small companies in the town. Dr. Tom Stanback came to Spencer in 1911 to manage the new Rowan Drug Company and began selling a formula for headaches and sickness which he had invented. The product was so successful that he enlarged his business to a building on Fifth Street and employed box folders and salesmen. During the 20 years the business operated in Spencer, Stanback Headache Powders became a regional household name, and Stanback eventually moved to larger facilities in Salisbury. John H. Gobbel and Sons ran a grist mill in Spencer for four years beginning in 1919, but it never became a large concern. The Catawba Ice and Fuel Company, which began in East Spencer in 1912, provided ice for boxcars but hired only a modest number of part-time employees. The large industries hoped for by Spencer's leaders never materialized, and the town remained vulnerable in its great dependency on the shops.

Roundhouse nameplate on north end of the building.

This Sept. 29, 1946, view, from near the area of the Spencer depot, shows the great amount of smoke that emanated from the engines and work at the shops. Note the footbridge for pedestrian traffic between Spencer and East Spencer.

North Carolina Division of Archives and History

In the late 1940s Spencer Shops continued in its prime. This view shows the town with its Southern-provided park across from the shops, the heart of the industrial complex, and the freight yard.

Ties *magazine*

Machinist J. C. Moore runs a Newton vertical milling machine with a Turehan follower attachment.

The Spencer Worker

6

World War II marked the peak of employment at the Spencer Shops and terminal. It also marked the earliest stages of the diesel era, in which shopmen would find their work changing in a way they could never have imagined. This is a good point, then, to take a closer look at Spencer workers and their work experience. The tasks and procedures discussed here pertain to the steam era in general and the 1930s and 1940s in particular. While new machines and equipment were continuously being introduced to raise efficiency (some machines were actually invented at Spencer), the basic division of labor and work procedures was relatively static in the steam age.

The best place to begin an analysis of work at Spencer is with the various workers and craftsmen at the shops. Many trainmen (engineers, firemen, brakemen, and conductors) were also based at Spencer, and a description of their work is included. None of these trainmen worked at the shops site itself except for hostlers, engineers who operated locomotives in the shop yard. Some trainmen, especially brakemen, sorted cars in the freight yard, but most worked on many trains that departed daily for destinations 20 to 200 miles away. Trainmen's work is better known than that of shopmen, so the descriptions will be much briefer. All played an essential part in making the Spencer Shops and yard Southern's largest and most active terminal for much of the steam era.

Shop Managers and Supervisors

The management hierarchy at Spencer changed periodically, and the tasks of each position fluctuated. All officials at the shops were supervised by the superintendent of motive power, who controlled train movements across Southern Railway's eastern lines. The superintendent usually kept an office at Charlotte but periodically stopped at Spencer on inspection tours.

For much of the steam period the highest mechanical department official at Spencer Shops was the master mechanic, who was responsible for keeping locomotives and rail cars at Spencer and surrounding areas in good condition. In early years the dis-

David Driscoll/SRHA collection

Roundhouse foremen pose for a portrait on Sept. 29, 1946. Second from left is the beloved Bob Julian.

A machinist operates a verticle lathe in the back shop.

Ties *magazine*

trict for which Spencer master mechanics were responsible stretched from Spencer north to Monroe, Virginia, 168 miles away on the main line. Later, especially during the diesel era, the master mechanic's jurisdiction covered a much larger area. With diesels fewer terminals, shops, and locomotives were needed to carry out railroad operations, and one master mechanic directed an area which had once required several men. The master mechanic oversaw all inspection and maintenance activity at the shops. He traveled occasionally to other terminals within his district to inspect facilities or solve repair problems. He had to respond quickly to any nearby train wreck to clear the track as soon as possible. The master mechanic also filled vacancies at the shops.

The master mechanic carried tremendous responsibility. Difficult decisions could make him the most loved or most hated man at the shops. At least one master mechanic angered Spencer workers to the extent that it cost him his job. In January 1905 J. F. Sheehan became master mechanic, replacing popular S. R. Richards, who joined another company. Sheehan's brusque style and anti-union attitudes alienated shopmen. "The unions are running things too much out here, and I'm going to break it up," he reportedly said, which put workers on edge.

A confrontation soon came. On January 27 the sun rose over the coldest day of the year. The wind cut sharply through the craftsmen as they trudged to the roundhouse. When they got there the small heating stoves between the stalls were cold and quiet, and the coal used for fuel was nowhere to be seen. From his office, Sheehan reported that the coal had been taken away as an economy measure. It was just too expensive to use as fuel, he claimed. The shopmen cursed Sheehan through chattering teeth and contemplated a strike. Perhaps remembering a recent failed strike by the machinists, they decided instead to send a delegation to Southern headquarters in Washington to complain. While the delegation was en route, Carl Hammer, editor of the *Salisbury Sun*, printed stories and editorials depicting Sheehan as an uncompromising ogre.

In early February Sheehan and his assistant, M. A. Shank, stormed into Hammer's office and demanded that the paper cease its negative reporting. Hammer ordered the infuriated master mechanic out of his office, whereupon Sheehan bashed the hapless editor over the head with his fist. Shank ushered his boss out before further violence occurred, but Sheehan was later fined $5 for assault and $10 for trespassing. Hammer responded by learning, and then printing, that the coal used in the roundhouse stoves had cost the railroad nothing. It had been waste coal picked up around the yard by laborers.

Upon hearing the roundhouse workers' complaints, the railway sent an agent to investigate. He ordered the coal returned to the roundhouse

Ties *magazine*

Forging an eccentric crank arm in the blacksmith shop. Left to right: blacksmith J. W. Clements, heater Rob Holt, helper Tom Durham, and hammerman Bill Carr.

stoves. He also ordered construction of a "warming room" where workers could thaw their hands and feet on particularly cold days. In April the railroad sent Sheehan to another location. His three-month tenure, the shortest of any master mechanic at Spencer, was unusual. Most of the master mechanics at Spencer weren't hated. Their high management positions made them natural targets of worker anger, but workers also realized that the master mechanics always did what they felt was in the best interest of the company.

The shop superintendent was the second highest official at the shops. He supervised heavy repair and overhaul work in the back shop and in the blacksmith and boiler shops. The superintendent made sure that work progressed smoothly and correctly. He also tried to make repair and overhaul procedures more efficient and economical.

Each department at the shops had a general foreman with several shift foremen under him. Foremen made sure that work progressed at a sensible pace and met company standards. Shift foremen often came to work a half hour early to meet with foremen on the preceding shift and learn about work in progress.

Most foremen had served as craftsmen for years and occupied peculiar positions between management and labor. They explained the managerial view to workers and also brought workers' concerns to the attention of management. Foremen also fired men for performing poorly or breaking company rules. If an employee felt that he had been dismissed unjustly, he could request a hearing, with union and company officials present, in which the foreman had to justify the dismissal.

There also were assistant foremen in each department, and many foremen had been assistants. They took correspondence school courses and attended company training seminars before and after becoming foremen. The training kept them abreast of new maintenance techniques and dif-

ferent situations they would encounter in the daily operation of the shops.

Inspectors, also often former craftsmen, made official inspections of each locomotive which arrived at the site. They examined locomotives in the roundhouse and on the inspection tracks beside the oil house, listing needed repairs for each locomotive on cards which they sent to the roundhouse office. A team of car inspectors also scoured the freight yard for damaged rail cars.

In addition to this regular maintenance, federal law required detailed periodic examinations of locomotive components, such as boilers, which could be dangerous if they malfunctioned. Inspectors at Spencer were careful to make timely examinations and fill out forms correctly because the shops could be shut down by the Interstate Commerce Commission if inspection procedures were not followed precisely. Federal agents might also show up unexpectedly at any time for surprise inspections.

Ties *magazine*

Unlike other craftsmen, electricians would be in great demand with the advent of diesels. Electrician G. A Walton tests a voltage regulator on a test bench designed and built at Spencer.

Craftsmen

A craftsmen was a person skilled in a recognized shop craft. He generally had been an apprentice for two to four years. Each craft had a separate national union. By 1918 unions and railroads had worked out agreements which put every repair task in the specific jurisdiction of one of the crafts. If a craftsman was caught performing a repair in the jurisdiction of another craft, he could be fined or even lose his job. This division of labor among crafts was stringently enforced and broken up only with the arrival of diesels which required very different repair procedures. A description of the duties of craftsmen at Spencer Shops follows.

Machinists: Practitioners of this craft operated machine tools, power-driven machines used to form metal into desired shapes. Some machinists manufactured parts using machine tools such as turret lathes or planers while others worked directly on locomotives. In the back shop a number of machinists worked at a single machine tool all day, turning out common parts such as bolts or piston rods in assembly-line fashion. Others used machines to shape specific parts for particular locomotives.

Machinists who worked directly with locomotives in the back shop were sometimes called "floor machin-ists." They maintained locomotive parts and components, such as driving rods, connecting rods, crossheads and guides, cylinders, pistons, wheels, and axles, which were not under the domain of other craftsmen. Teams of machinists, helpers, and apprentices (see below) inspected, removed, machined, and replaced the parts. With the help of the blacksmith department, machinists could make whatever tools they needed to complete a repair job. As part of their apprenticeships machinists made their own small hand tools, which they kept as personal possessions throughout their careers. Machinists were the most common craftsmen in the roundhouse and back shop and handled minor repairs and adjustments performed there.

Boilermakers: As the name implies, these craftsmen primarily reconditioned and replaced locomotive boilers. They fabricated or re-worked layers of stayed sheet metal which formed boilers and tested flues for blockages and leaks. They repaired (or built from scratch) fireboxes and brick arches along with the braces, rods, and stay bolts which supported these larger structures. Boilermakers also maintained water and air tanks, grates and ash pans, pilots(cowcatchers), steel cabs, and running boards. In their work boilermakers used welders, punches, shears, electric cutting and grinding machines, riveters, and bolt cutters. Larger machines in the boiler shop included bending rolls (which rolled flat pieces of metal into cylinders), flange presses, and multiple-spindle drills for drilling holes in flue and firebox sheets.

When a locomotive came into the back shop for overhaul, inspectors from the boiler shop carefully examined every item over which boilermakers had repair jurisdiction. For efficiency boilermakers performed minor repair and overhaul work in the back shop rather than remove parts and take them to the boiler shop. Only when large components, such as fireboxes, needed complete overhaul were they carted to the boiler shop. If these large pieces were worn or damaged severely, boilermakers often dismantled them, scrapped the metal, and made new replacements. They made most replacement parts from scratch using the machines and tools listed above. They even built completely new boilers, using drills and punching machines to make holes in firebox and smokebox sheets through which flues would pass. The flat sheets were then shaped using the bending roll machines and welding torches. Finally, completed boilers were moved to the back shop for installation in the proper locomotives.

Riveting was a big part of boilermaking before electric welding technology developed in the 1930s and 1940s. Boilermakers employed "rivet busters" and pneumatic (air-driven) wrenches to remove bolts and rivets which held locomotive parts together or in place. They used pneumatic rivet guns of various sizes to replace the bolts. Oxyacetylene torch welding eventually replaced many of the bolts and rivets, and the boilermakers adapted to the new technology.

In the diesel era boilermakers were forced to change their work drastically. Most of the repair jobs under their jurisdiction disappeared with the steam engine, but they continued to recondition diesel oil and water tanks and welded large parts, such as cracked or dented crankcases. Unfor-tunately for the boilermakers, the diesel repair tasks under their jurisdiction were never clearly defined. Machinists' skills were more easily adapted to diesel repair, and boilermakers often accused machinists of hoarding the new repair jobs. Animosity between the machinist and boilermaker unions reached national proportions and was still raging when Spencer Shops closed.

Blacksmiths: Spencer blacksmiths used large machines to forge heated metal into an infinite variety of shapes and sizes. Railroad blacksmiths produced driving and piston rods, crank pins, driving wheel axles, locomotive and rail car frames and trucks, rail car side bars and handles, and the heavy springs which served as shock absorbers for driving wheels. Blacksmiths also forged many tools made at the site and sent them to the back shop to be machined to exact size.

Large parts such as driving rods (which connected driving wheels on steam locomotives) arrived at the shops in raw form and had to be shaped and sized to fit the particular locomotive on which they were to be installed. Blacksmiths heated one end of a driving rod in a furnace, then beat it into shape using one of the large, steam-powered, vertical trip hammers in the blacksmith shop. The sound of these hammers hitting giant parts could be heard (and felt) in the town of Spencer hundreds of yards away. After one end of the driving rod had been pounded into shape, jib cranes turned the part so the other end could receive the same treatment. The operation required four workers: a heater who minded the furnace, a blacksmith who positioned the part so that it would be hammered correctly, a helper who assisted him, and a hammerman who operated the steam hammer.

When forging smaller parts, blacksmiths at Spencer did not fit the typical image of a man in an apron hammering a horseshoe on an anvil. Huge rectangular forging machines did the pounding, but blacksmiths still required great skill and knowledge to shape parts accurately with the machines. The action of the machine bent or compacted heated metal, an action also known as "upsetting."

To begin the upsetting process, the helper heated the part (or "blank") to be upset in a large furnace beside the forging machine. Using tongs, he removed the blank from the furnace and set it on a table between himself and the blacksmith. The latter then used his own tongs to pick up the blank and put the heated section in a slot in the front of the forging machine. The blacksmith then pressed a foot peddle, and two interchangeable clamps, called "gripping

North Carolina Division of Archives and History
Carmen repair a wooden boxcar at Spencer Shops.

dies," closed on the blank to hold it securely in place. The primary moving part of the machine, the "heading slide," then rammed down onto the end of the blank. The blacksmith had attached an interchangeable die to the heading slide which governed how the blank was bent or compacted when the heading slide hit it. In most cases the blacksmith changed the heading die and repeated the process until the blank was bent to the required shape. Parts shaped in forging machines

included driving and truck wheel springs, grab iron bars, stay and coupler pin bolts, draft keys, knuckle pin and castle nuts, and piston and cylinder rods.

The blacksmith shop was the recycling center at Spencer. Iron parts too worn to be repaired were heated and shaped into new parts or tools rather than thrown away. New and recycled parts and tools were tempered (by heating and sudden cooling) so they could take the punishment

White-collar workers, many of them clerks, spent countless hours in the master mechanic's office.

they would endure in operation.

Spencer blacksmiths did repair work in addition to manufacturing duties. If large parts such as driving rods or running boards became bent, blacksmiths straightened them by heating and pounding or by using a flattening machine called a "bulldozer." This repair work was restricted to certain tasks on certain parts, however, as most repair jobs fell under the jurisdiction of other crafts.

Until World War I blacksmiths did most of the welding done in the nation's railroad shops. As the use of oxyacetylene and other portable torches grew, other crafts complained that it was inefficient to wait for blacksmiths to do work which they could do themselves. In 1918 an arbitration board of the U.S. Department of Labor ruled that blacksmiths retained jurisdiction only over welding in which initially separate pieces of metal were joined together. The blacksmiths could take portable welders to locomotives in back shops or roundhouses and do this type of work. The board ruled, however, that welding to repair parts which had been worn or hollowed out could be done by the craft under whose repair jurisdiction those parts normally fell.

The ruling left a wide range of welding work for the blacksmiths, which helped them maintain at least some importance when diesels replaced steam engines. Blacksmiths welded or forged some of the more cumbersome diesel parts, such as frames and axles, and continued to forge car parts. Yet the number of jobs under their jurisdiction decreased substantially. By the time the blacksmith shop closed in 1960, the blacksmiths were experiencing a heavy loss of importance and prestige.

Electricians: In the steam era Spencer electricians did little to service locomotives except maintain headlights, marker lights, and the turbo-generators which powered them. The men found plenty to do, however, as they had jurisdiction over maintenance of the vast body of electrical equipment at the shops. They scoured the complex testing light fixtures, outlets, wiring, crane motors, and transformers. At least two electricians were in the powerhouse around the clock to monitor and service generators and electrical equipment. Still, electricians' numbers remained small when compared to the other crafts, and their work area was only a small section of the upstairs gallery of the back shop.

Ironically electricians were the only craftsmen whose job security increased upon the coming of the diesel locomotive. The first diesels arrived at Spencer with a maze of electric motors and circuitry, and the shops' management had to hire new electricians and train them in diesel maintenance. Electricians played an especially important role in diesel overhauls. They removed electrical parts and wiring from dismantled diesels in the back shop and carted them to the old flue shop building, which was converted to an electric shop around 1950. They tested wires and electrical components with devices largely designed and built in the shop. One helpful homemade device was a form board which allowed electricians to trace out a wiring circuit and inspect it for frayed wire or faulty connections.

If a particular apparatus was not working properly, electricians dismantled it and corrected the problem. Utilizing a supply of replacement parts kept in the shop, electricians rebuilt small electric motors, replaced faulty fuses and connections, and rewired electrical systems.

Spencer electricians even began handling especially difficult repairs to equipment at other shops on Southern's eastern lines. If the machines could not be fixed on the spot, the electricians took them back to their shop where they had more space to work and better equipment. They also repaired radios and walkie-talkies which, beginning in the 1950s, became the primary means of communication in the freight yard and among train crews.

Carmen: Carmen serviced all parts of freight and passenger rail cars. They worked with brake systems, wheels, wheel trucks, and the windows and doors of passenger cars. Carpenters and laborers in the woodworking shop were considered part of the car department. They used planing mills to cut logs into boards of various sizes for replacing worn-out boards in wooden boxcars. While installing new boards carpenters pounded incessantly with their hammers, so much that other shopmen called them "car knockers." The

Custom-made portable toolboxes sit near engines No. 1479, 1395, and 1376. The open toolbox has a simple safety slogan: "Get Your Goggles."

equipment in the woodworking shop and car sheds enabled carpenters to build wooden rail cars from scratch if desired, but Southern almost always bought new cars directly from manufacturers.

After the 1910s, wooden cars slowly became extinct, but carpenters continued to work on locomotive cabs because the windows, seats, doors, door locks, glass, and flooring fell under their jurisdiction. They also kept busy building wooden carts, shanties for roadmen, and window frames for passenger cars. The cab work continued until the arrival of diesels with all-metal cabs.

Typical duties carman learned after the advent of steel rail cars included welding, riveting, and operating cutting torches. Using hand tools and heavy machines in their shop, carmen could shorten or lengthen cars, strengthen them with metal support beams, or change their basic structure. In the late 1950s, Spencer carmen took on the enormous task of converting Southern's aging fleet of 40-foot boxcars into open pulpwood cars. They stripped each car to its frame and rebuilt it. After installing new flooring and building bulkheads at each end of a car, the carmen added heavier wheels and braking systems. Most overhauls and heavy repairs involved freight cars. Passenger cars received minor repairs at Spencer, but most heavy passenger car work ended up at Southern's Hayne car shop in Spartanburg, South Carolina.

Several carmen were inspectors in the Spencer freight yard. They helped brakemen attach the air hoses of cars in trains which had been made up and were ready to leave the yard. Then the inspectors signaled the engineer in the locomotive to put on his brakes so that they could determine if the air brakes on each car were hooked up properly and fully functional. Inspectors also examined journal (axle) bearings and coupling units on cars. Carmen referred to any car needing repairs as a "bad order" car. Switch engines moved bad order cars to a special track leading into the car shop.

Painters: Painters handled all painting required in rolling stock repair and general maintenance of shop buildings. The painters usually had a building all to themselves where they spray-painted locomotives and rail cars. They took care of smaller jobs to locomotive cabs, tenders, and rail cars in the shop buildings where these items were repaired. These small jobs usually involved detailing or lettering, a job experienced painters could do by hand without stencils. Painters spent much time painting and repainting the interiors and exteriors of buildings. The huge safety slo-

The train crew of light Pacific passenger locomotive No. 1211 poses for a photo. Note the eagle and candlesticks adorning the headlight.

gans on each end of the back shop, for example, were the handiwork of painters.

Pipefitters, Sheet Metal Workers, and Tinsmiths: Pipe-fitters and sheet metal workers were in the same union because pipes on many locomotives before 1900 were made of copper and repaired by coppersmiths in the sheet metal workers' union. Even though the metal on piping changed over the years, the pipefitters never formed a separate union. Pipefitters serviced and replaced all piping on locomotives except flue pipes which were cared for by boilermakers.

Sheet metal workers dealt only with very thin metal, specifically less than 16-gauge. This narrow jurisdiction kept the number of sheet metal workers small, but those at Spencer stayed busy soldering and welding various parts of locomotives and tenders and any thin metal in the shop buildings. Many of them also worked with babbit, a soft metal alloy used in bearings and pistons.

During locomotive overhauls in the back shop, tinsmiths, who were also in the sheet metal workers' union, removed, repaired, and replaced metal sheets surrounding boilers. The tinsmiths had to work fast, for further dismantling of boilers could not proceed until they had removed the covering sheets. No one in any other craft could remove the sheets, for that would have been a violation of craft jurisdiction.

Helpers, Laborers, Apprentices, and Clerks

Workers neither management nor craftsmen were also essential to the shops: they were helpers, laborers, apprentices, or clerks.

Helpers were generally assigned to assist craftsman. The helpers' work was almost always physical, much of it unskilled. A helper carried large tools and spare parts for a craftsman and often pushed his personal tool cart. Helpers working with machinists and boilermakers held parts while the craftsman worked on them or helped him move cumbersome parts to a work area. Some parts on steam engines were removed by putting a wedge next to them and hammering the wedge until the part fell out. The craftsman (usually a floor machinist) held the wedge while the helper hammered. A helper who was a strong and accurate hammerer was held in high esteem by machinists. Some helpers became apprentices and eventually gained craftsman status, but most did not. One reason was that many helpers were blacks who, until Spencer closed, were not allowed to become craftsmen. White helpers who apprenticed often had their terms reduced from four to two years because of knowledge they had gained as helpers. They could also reduce the apprenticeship by taking correspondence courses.

Emergency labor shortages, in protracted strikes or wartime, often resulted in helpers being "set up" temporarily to perform the duties of a craftsman without completing, or sometimes even starting, an apprenticeship. The "set up" ended when the crisis was over. Retired Spencer shopmen claim there were occasions when a craftsman came down with unexpected illness and his helper was asked to take his place until another craftsman could be called in. Officially, Spencer management denied that this situation ever occurred.

Laborers performed physical labor not assigned to craftsmen or helpers, and tasks varied from department to department. Laborers attempted to keep buildings at Spencer clean, a herculean task by any standard. They swept and mopped, loaded trash and waste onto wagons, and then carted it off.

Teams of wipers polished locomotives at the roundhouse. Small groups worked at the cinder pits and coal chutes, filling locomotives and tenders with sand, coal, and water and cleaning cinders from ash pans. Workers in the cattle pens and transfer sheds were also usually laborers. Seniority lists enabled long-time laborers to keep the higher-paying positions. Though laborers received the lowest wages of any permanent employees at the shops, they earned more than unskilled workers in other area industries.

An apprentice was anyone training to become a craftsman. The training normally lasted four to five years unless the trainee had been a helper whereupon the time might be cut to as little as two years.

At least once monthly apprentices attended on-site classes in their crafts conducted by Southern instructors who traveled from shop to shop. Apprentices paid for these classes but also earned regular wages during their apprenticeships.

The most valuable information apprentices learned came not in classrooms but on the shop floor. Here veteran craftsmen taught unofficial labor-saving techniques and showed apprentices that it was essential to have a "feel" for the nature of metal. The master craftsmen were not averse to teasing while they taught. Machinists would tell an apprentice to cut a bolt or small tool without explaining that metals expand due to heat produced in machining. As a result, the apprentice's first product often would be the wrong size when finished, if it were finished at all. An apprentice might crack parts while machining them or produce something bearing no resemblance at all to what he was supposed to be making. Experienced craftsmen hooted with laughter, but the apprentices learned valuable lessons about shop work. They discovered that one learned more by doing than by reading a book and that instinct, gained only from experience, was the most valuable tool of a craftsman.

Apprentices in the back shop sometimes retaliated against particularly odious craftsmen by sabotaging their tools or dousing them with water from the upstairs gallery. Overall, though, relations between craftsmen and apprentices were cordial because nepotism was a factor at the shops, and craftsmen often knew and worked with relatives of their apprentices.

Clerks at Spencer handled filing, record keeping, and other paperwork. In addition to clerks, timekeepers, stenographers, telephone switchboard operators, and telegraphers staffed the main office and payroll department which took up almost a third of the largest storage building. Clerks also worked in the boilershop, roundhouse, car shed, storehouse, and yardmaster's office. In the roundhouse and car department clerks kept inspection records and helped allocate work assignments to craftsmen. Storehouse clerks kept meticulous records of items used so that proper re-orders could be made. Clerks in the yardmaster's office kept records on individual rail cars and drew up orders for train crews.

The work of clerks was considered

This was the look of early diesels at Spencer and their proud crews. With engineer W. J. Stadler of Spencer in the gangway, engines No. 4148, 4332, and 4152 pose on March 23, 1947.

so important that some were paid more than craftsmen. Clerical positions were also the only ones open to women at the shops proper.

Trainmen

Southern classified inspection and repair work at its shops under the mechanical department, while operation of trains fell under the transportation department. Each department had separate unions, seniority lists, management structures, and wage scales. Trainmen and shopmen at Spencer rarely had contact with each other on the job, but off the job they were neighbors who sent their children to the same schools and belonged to the same churches and community organizations.

Engineers: From their perch inside locomotives, engineers controlled train speeds and carefully observed signals along the track which indicated conditions ahead. Engineers also oiled and lubricated locomotive parts while out on runs. Operating a locomotive took great skill, and engineers were well compensated for their knowledge. Theirs was the highest paying non-supervisory position in railroading. They also needed enough mechanical knowledge so that if their locomotive broke down on the line they could make the repairs necessary to get it to the near-

est terminal.

Firemen: In the steam era firemen kept fires in locomotive fireboxes hot by feeding them fuel (usually coal). Firemen also made sure locomotives had enough water, helped engineers look out for signals, and learned all they could about engineering in hopes of eventual promotion. Before each run firemen checked to see that locomotive cabs were supplied with drinking water, small tools, and lubricating oil. When trains stopped enroute, firemen might help engineers oil moving parts and spot-check for damage but usually were busy clearing debris from cabs and helping take on coal and water.

Firemen might work 15 years or more before an engineer's position became available. For most of the time that trains ran out of Spencer, black firemen could not be promoted to engineer due to union rules. Spencer retirees remember seeing black firemen become engineers for the first time in the 1970s.

Hostlers: Hostlers operated switching locomotives in the shop area, pushing dead locomotives around the shops and into roundhouse stalls. Hostling was the work of firemen and often was a step in training they took to become engineers. Hostlers worked regular eight-hour shifts and did not leave the shops. At

Attentive men in the yard tower control traffic in and out of the Spencer yard. Their job is akin to air traffic controllers at airports.

one time 21 hostlers were employed at Spencer, seven on each shift.

Brakemen: In the early days of railroading brakemen operated hand brakes on top of rail cars. Icy weather and low bridges made the job particularly dangerous, though new engineer-controlled air brakes had virtually eliminated that danger by the time the Spencer terminal opened in 1896.

On passenger trains brakemen made sure that heating and lighting mechanisms worked properly. On both freight and passenger trains brakemen were in charge of flag and light signals on the front and rear of trains. If a train made an unplanned or emergency stop, the brakeman walked back down the track at least half a mile and placed flags, flares, or torpedoes on the track to warn approaching trains that a train was stopped ahead. Some trains had a flagman who did this type of signalling and flagging.

On freight trains brakemen assisted with coupling and uncoupling cars and occasionally with loading freight. When trains were stopping or starting or having more cars coupled to them, brakemen signaled engineers to go forward or backward with arm or lantern signals. The range of movement in the signals indicated the speed at which engineers were to execute the motion. Brakemen's other duties included disembarking from trains to throw track switches and helping conductors keep records on cars in trains. Experience for new brakemen was acquired "on the job," and it was essential that they become familiar with their normal stretch of track to anticipate problems and be ready to work quickly at sidings and switching yards.

Conductors: Conductors could be considered the captains of trains. They took orders from yardmasters and dispatchers as to their trains' movements and destinations. On

freight trains conductors oversaw switching of cars and loading and unloading of less-than-carload freight. On passenger trains conductors collected fares from passengers and looked after their comfort and welfare. Conductors gave orders to engineers, who were usually paid more than they were, a fact Spencer retirees remember with humor.

Yardmasters: Yardmasters supervised freight classification yards and transfer sheds. They planned the make-up of trains and directed the coupling and uncoupling of groups of cars on trains in the yard. They gave orders to engineers of switch engines, yard brakemen, and conductors. Yardmasters also made sure the complicated clerical work in the yard office ran smoothly. With trains arriving constantly, Spencer yardmasters ensured that classification and switching of cars was done efficiently. If work in the yard was too slow, the yard might overflow with cars, causing delays in train schedules. Yardmasters also made sure safety procedures were followed in the freight yard, railroading's most notorious arena for accidents because of passing locomotives and constantly shifting cars.

Runs From the Spencer Yard

For much of the time that the Spencer freight yard operated, trainmen could bid on four types of train run. "Chain gang" runs involved dead, or extra, freight. They occurred only when enough freight had accumulated at the site to make up a trainload. "Carded" runs moved high priority freight on a regular schedule. These runs often were to Asheville or Goldsboro, North Carolina; Greenville, South Carolina; or Monroe, Virginia. The trip to Monroe was a typical main line run. In the steam era it took around 13

Richard Patton/Marvin Rogers and Paul Hess Collection
Freight locomotive No. 4907 leaves the Spencer yard with a fresh crew in September 1947.

hours to travel to Monroe. After giving the train to a crew who would take it to Washington, the Spencer crew rested at the Monroe YMCA until they took over a train going south and back to Spencer.

"Local freight" runs covered the surrounding area. Thomasville and Lexington, each less than 25 miles away, were common destinations. These runs did not require that trainmen be away from home for extended times. Passenger runs, like non-local freight runs, often took crews to Monroe, Asheville, Goldsboro, or Greenville, where they stayed over until they took a train headed back to Spencer. Federal legislation giving trainmen an eight-hour regular workday had been part of the Adamson Act of 1916. Before then railroads did not have to give trainmen a certain number of hours to rest between runs.

Trainmen from other terminals who had layovers at Spencer stayed in the YMCA or boarding houses near the shops. For many years call boys ran from the yard office and roundhouse to the boarding houses to retrieve needed train crews. Luther Ellis Burch, a retired railroader, recalled his start as a call boy at Spencer in 1904. Street lights in Spencer were scarce at that time and at night the boys carried lanterns through the dark streets on their way to wake sleeping trainmen. In those

years the railroad sometimes called crews back to work only two or three hours after they had finished a run. Burch would go into the room of a sleeping conductor or engineer, light his lamp, and shake him till he stirred. The man signed a book indicating that he had been called, and Burch's job was finished.

Some trainmen were not happy to see Burch, especially if they had had little sleep or had been drinking. "I had some fella draw a gun on me one time," he recalled.

"He'd been uptown. It was when they had saloons in Salisbury, and I think he was about half shot, and he hadn't been to bed about an hour or so. I kept poking at the window and he said 'get away from there' and reached under his pillow and drew out a gun. Boy I left, went back to report to the foreman, you know, what he'd done. They sent another man for him and finally got him out of there. He admitted doing it, but he wasn't conscious what he was doing, I think. They disqualified him for the run, because he was intoxicated."

Burch faced other guns and even had his lantern shot out on one occasion, but such incidents were rare.

Many trainmen, married ones in particular, spent their layovers thinking more about getting home than about getting drunk. Engineers from Spencer were known to give a special sequence of blasts on their locomotive whistles as they approached town at the end of a long, overnight run to let their wives know they were returning. A hot bath and a hot meal awaited them at home. For most trainmen, no further recompense was required.

Jim Wrinn
Volunteers who later put Spencer Shops back on track as a museum often came out of devotion to a place where they'd spent most of their lives. Here veteran Southern employees H. S. Williams (left), an engineer, and Milton Ruble, a foreman, struggle with a steam locomotive part.

North Carolina Division of Archives and History
2-8-0 locomotive No. 444 rests in the roundhouse. Note the jack under the pilot.

Following a Locomotive Through Inspection and Repair

7

An examination of the service, inspection, and repairs given to a locomotive from the moment it entered the Spencer yard and shops to the moment it left shows how every position from craftsman to laborer was essential in keeping the locomotive fleet in top condition. Steam locomotives were inspected every 150 to 200 service miles, so a train rarely stopped at Spencer without switching locomotives. Brakemen uncoupled the locomotive from the train upon arrival at the yard. The engineer then ran the locomotive to the shops via a track known as the "roundhouse lead." Leads from both ends of the yard accommodated locomotives coming from either direction. The north lead ran by the west side of the master mechanic's office while the south lead circled around the coal chute. Both led to inspection tracks near the roundhouse. Passenger locomotives were uncoupled at the Spencer or Salisbury depots, then brought by the engineer or a hostler via the leads to the inspection tracks. Here inspectors made a point- by-point examination of the undercarriage and exterior moving parts of each locomotive. Pits beneath the tracks allowed inspectors to walk under a locomotive. An onlooker might see only an inspector's head poking from the pit, his eyes intently searching for damage. The inspector filled out a form for each

locomotive and noted any problems. The form went to the roundhouse office with a written record of any defects the locomotive's crew had detected during its run.

A hostler then took the locomotive to the cinder pits at the south end of the shops. Here laborers scraped burning cinders and coal from the firebox through grates into ash pans beneath it. They used pressurized water to cool the coals quickly to avoid burning the ash pan. They then used the water and rakes to scrape the ashes and cinders into pits below the

David Driscoll/SRHA collection

2-8-2 locomotive No. 4803 sits on blocks in the back shop during overhaul with wheels and many other parts removed in 1949.

rails. Laborers who performed these tasks were known as "fire-knockers."

Though there was no fire in the firebox, the locomotive had enough steam left in the boiler for a hostler to run it to the wash track by the roundhouse. Here laborers cleaned the locomotive with an 180-degree mixture of water and solvents sprayed from a high-pressure hose. Laborers known

as "wipers" hand-cleaned the top of the locomotive, the cab, and any surfaces the hot water solution could not reach.

A hostler then used the turntable to direct the locomotive and its tender into a roundhouse stall. A locomotive usually had enough steam left to reach the roundhouse under its own power. If not, a "goat," or switch engine, pushed it. Unless it was to be immediately assigned to a run after inspection, the steam in the boiler was "bled," or slowly siphoned off. Workers also drained any hot water remaining in the boiler. If the steam or water was released too quickly, the metal might contract, causing serious structural damage. The hot water from the boiler was filtered and used to wash out or fill boilers of other locomotives.

While a locomotive was in the roundhouse, shopmen completed its inspection. They crawled into the still hot firebox to check for cracks in the metal and for faulty staybolts, the metal bars separating the boiler from the firebox. This was very dangerous as heat in the firebox could damage lungs or cause a man to lose consciousness. Inspectors entered the smokebox in front of the locomotive to check for damage and also examined running gear, air and water pumps, lights, and piping systems. Any problems discovered were added to the locomotive's repair record.

No. 1554, a shop switcher takes on water at Spencer Shops roundhouse. The engine was used to shuttle dead locomotives around the shop area.

The roundhouse foreman scheduled locomotive repairs after consultation with the freight yard office, giving priority to locomotives used on the most common runs and on unscheduled, or "extra," runs. Clerks in the office at the back of the roundhouse filled out forms, called "tickets," listing repairs for each locomotive. The clerks sorted the tickets in pigeonholes in a wall cabinet. Each craftsman took a ticket from the hole labeled for his craft and the type of locomotive (passenger or freight) he worked with. After the craftsman and his helper completed the repair indicated on the ticket, he signed it, left it for the foreman to pick up, and returned to the office for another assignment.

The most common types of craftsmen in the roundhouse were machinists, boilermakers, and pipefitters. Each craftsmen generally worked on specific parts of certain locomotives. One machinist might repair running gear on freight locomotives from the Danville Division (all track between Spencer and Monroe, Virginia). Another might work on air brakes or water pumps on passenger locomotives on the Asheville Division (from Spencer to Asheville). The roundhouse operated on three eight-hour shifts and never closed. Each shift had workers from each craft assigned to both passenger and freight locomotives. On rare occasions when the yard office needed a certain locomotive quickly, a foreman could request that a craftsman leave his work and help others at that particular locomotive. Craftsmen cursed disruption in their routine but usually complied.

The variety of repairs in the roundhouse seems endless. Possible repairs to boiler components included renewing stay and crown bolts, caulking seams, and replacing flues and flue sheets. Work on firing mechanisms included repairing ash pans and front-end netting and replacing brick in fireboxes. Repairs to running gear, machinery, and accessories might include renewing rod brasses, pistons, and valve rings; re-boring cylinders and valve chambers; replacing tires and wheels; repairing springs, spring rigging, driving boxes, valves, and steam lines; and renewing superheater units. Minor defects in smokestacks, brakes, and cab accessories such as gauges, water columns, firedoors, and reverse gears also received attention in the roundhouse. Repairs requiring only a few hours were made in the stall in which the locomotive initially parked. If the repairs required several days, hostlers moved the locomotive to one of the first three stalls where it could be kept a couple of weeks if necessary.

Until the late 1940s, when the roundhouse was converted to allow repair of diesel locomotives, the room at the back of the roundhouse con-

This locomotive is set up on blocks for overhaul in the back shop with its wheels and motion work removed.

tained a small machine shop. Parts to be machined (smoothed, straightened, or changed in size) often ended up there. Parts requiring extensive machining, however, were usually taken to the back shop. If the parts were large, the roundhouse's overhead cranes carried them to a back door in stall four or seven. A large outdoor crane then carried the parts via a craneway to the back shop. On the way the crane dipped the parts in a lye pit to cleanse them of grease and oil.

Interchangeable components such as air pumps, safety valves, gauges, truck wheels, electric generators, and air-brake equipment were generally replaced instead of repaired. Some of these parts could be mass-produced in the back shop, and roundhouse workers kept a large supply on hand. Craftsmen often had to machine even these "interchangeable" parts to install them properly. Manufacturers generally built each steam locomotive to specifications supplied by the buyer, which meant locomotives of the same model could have slightly different parts. As a locomotive underwent overhauls over the years, its parts would be altered or replaced with whatever was on hand at a particular shop. A 20-year-old locomotive might resemble Frankenstein's monster: a lumbering behemoth fashioned of old parts, none of them original. This kept shopmen busy shaping parts to fit individual steam locomotives. A primary reason diesel locomotives later replaced steam engines was their truly interchangeable parts, which saved railroads time and money.

Wheels were an example of "interchangeable" steam engine parts replaced in the roundhouse. The outermost bands of metal on the wheels, often called "tires," were also frequently replaced. Drop pits used in changing wheel sets ran under stalls three through eight. Hostlers aligned

David Driscoll/SRHA collection

Tenders were often separated from locomotives and sent to the tender repair shop while locomotives went to the back shop for overhaul. This photo was made in September 1946.

locomotives in these stalls so that the wheel set to be dropped sat directly over the pit. Workmen removed the running gear while a wheeled hydraulic jack ran along rails in the pit until it was aligned under the appropriate wheel set. Workers raised the piston of the jack until it met the wheel axle. After they removed the section of rail the wheels were sitting on, the jack lowered the wheel set into the pit. The jack moved the wheel set along the pit, then raised it back to

track level in stalls four or seven. The tracks in these stall led out the back of the roundhouse to wheel presses used to remove wheels from their axles. If wheels needed resurfacing, the outside crane transported them to the Back shop for machining. Workmen heated the tires, causing them to expand and be easier to remove. This was done at the wheel press station, or, if the wheels were small, at the drop pits. At the pits, workers used a circular torch which fit around a tire to heat it until

David Driscoll/SRHA collection

Drivers from steam locomotives wait near the wheel lathe for turning to normal contours. The large set at the left is marked with chalk for engine No. 4860 while that at the right is marked for No. 4812.

Superheater tubes protrude from the smokebox of this locomotive under overhaul in the back shop in 1948. A worker scrawled upside down on the piston cylinder, "For Governor: Vote for Jess James. Good as any."

it expanded and could be pried loose from the wheel.

From minor adjustments of crossheads to replacement of air pumps, the myriad of repairs promised there would be no idle moments. Grime-covered roundhouse craftsmen performed miracles on a daily basis and quickly prepared locomotives to return to service. When repairs had been completed, laborers refilled the boiler with hot water, shortening time needed to raise steam once the fire in the firebox was rekindled. If necessary, extra steam was pumped into the locomotive from a direct connection to boilers in the shops' powerhouse. Once it was under fire, hostlers guided the locomotive outside to the wash track where wipers again swarmed over it, cleaning and polishing the paint and metal to make it appear as close to new as possible. The railroad company required that wipers be much more meticulous with passenger locomo-

tives because they were more visible to the public.

A hostler then took the locomotive to the coal chute at the south end of the shops to receive coal, water, and sand. Sometimes a locomotive stopped at the scale house near the "ready tracks" where sensitive scales determined if the wheels were properly balanced. Like automobile wheels, locomotive wheels must be balanced for a smooth ride. The final stop for many locomotives was the ready tracks between the roundhouse and coal chute where they waited briefly until needed by the transportation department.

When starting a run, the engineer of a freight locomotive picked it up from the ready tracks (or the roundhouse if he needed it on short notice) and took it to the freight yard to be coupled to a train while the rest of the crew boarded. Hostlers took passenger locomotives to the Spencer or Salisbury depots where the crews boarded. Before they left on runs, crews often obtained small blocks of ice from the ice house, a small building beside the inspection tracks. The ice provided drinking water during a grueling 12 or 16-hour run.

Overhaul Procedure

A line of locomotives sits partially disassembled north of the back shop amidst an array of parts scattered on the ground.

Locomotives which were wrecked or needed heavy repairs were sent to the back shop instead of the roundhouse. Sometimes a locomotive was moved to the back shop if the repairs proved too much for the small machines in the roundhouse. Most locomotives entering the back shop, however, were undergoing scheduled overhauls. To begin the process, a locomotive (minus its tender) was pushed into the south end of the back shop. The locomotive was "dead," with no fire in the firebox and no water in the boiler. During the overhaul, the locomotive moved through the west side of the building, known as the "erecting shop." The locomotive entered on a central "communication track" which ran the entire length of the back shop. It stopped only a few feet into the building at the stripping pit. Here shopmen removed and inspected the locomotive's motion work which included rods, pistons, and connecting parts. Pits under the track allowed shopmen to get below the locomotive and disconnect the pedestal binders which held it to its wheels. Heavy cranes then lifted the locomotive off its wheels and placed it on blocks on one of two erecting tracks which flanked the communication track. When the back shop first opened, each erecting track held 12 locomotives, though this number decreased later as locomotives grew larger and longer.

While the locomotive was on the erecting track, shopmen removed all parts down to the boiler and frame. The shopmen marked each part to indicate its source and inspected it for wear. Parts in excellent shape were put temporarily in storage pits beside the communication track. Those needing repair received it in the machine shop (the east side of the back shop) or in the blacksmith, boiler, and flue shops depending on which craft had jurisdiction over that part. The balcony, or

North Carolina Division of Archives and History

A machinist uses a portable boring machine to smooth the inside of a cylinder. He brought the machine to the locomotive instead of removing the part and carrying it to the machine shop.

second floor of the machine shop, contained small departments which serviced water pumps and headlights. Other parts were turned and reconditioned on lathes and shaping and planing machines crowding the main floor of the shop.

New parts could often be made on the premises. As in the roundhouse, interchangeable parts could be replaced from stock in the back shop or storehouse. Some replacement parts were ordered from locomotive manufacturers, but others were produced en masse on lathes and other machines in the machine shop. This boring, repetitive labor was often done by apprentices who gained valuable machining experience. When all repaired parts were returned, new specialty parts made, and any physical changes to a locomotive's frame completed, the shopmen reconstructed the locomotive piece-by-piece on the

What a grand sight inside the back shop filled with steam locomotives. On June 13, 1948, Southern was buying diesels but still fixing steam locomotives. In the foreground are Nos. 764 and 5046. In the back shop are some engines visible and others parked in other sections of the shop: Nos. 4876, 2210, 4849, 595, 385, 4824, 4835, 4511, 5068, 6251, 1386, 1396, 1390, 1876, and 1270.

Switchers moved overhauled locomotives from the back shop to the firing-up shed for testing. 0-6-0T switcher No. 1595 wears a modern paint scheme in 1951, typically showing the pride the shop workers held in "their" locomotives.

erecting track. Cranes then picked the locomotive up, moved it to the communication track, and set it on its wheels, which had been refurbished on special lathes. Once all moving parts were lubricated, switchers pulled the locomotive out the north end of the back shop. During overhaul, all craftsmen who worked on a certain locomotive signed a form telling who had performed which tasks.

The rebuilt locomotive stopped just north of the back shop at the firing-up shed. Laborers filled the boiler with water and re-kindled the fire in its firebox. The fire was built up slowly because heating the water too quickly put undue stress on the boiler metal. A man known as an "engine tamer" then took the locomotive for a test run north of the shop site. The engine tamer and his fireman noted any problems the locomotive developed on the test run. When the locomotive returned, a foreman called the men who had worked on the defective parts to correct the problem if they were available. Retired Spencer shopmen smile when they recall certain craftsmen who, when told to re-do their work, explained to the foreman that the repair had been performed correctly the first time and that only an idiot could not tell a good repair from a bad one.

Once all problems had been corrected, the locomotive might be repainted. This was especially true of passenger locomotives, which Southern wanted to look immaculate at all times. After painting, a hostler took the locomotive to the coal chute for sand, coal, and water. He then guided it to the ready tracks to await its next assignment. During the back shop's early years a complete locomotive overhaul took 30 days. Technological innovations decreased this time substantially over the years.

Spencer Style
Not All Steam Locomotives Were Equal

Dale A. Roberts

Eagles, custom-built number plates, Masonic emblems, deer antlers, and other ornaments found their way onto engines. Some engineers made their own whistles or had friendly machinists create them.

As years went by, the head supervisor or master mechanic at each shop and his crew of workers began to customize locomotives assigned to their shop. As locomotives went through several shoppings over two or three decades, regional and individual styles emerged. Details such as handrails, outside cab fixtures, headlights, bells, and whistles varied from shop to shop. No two Southern steam engines matched exactly — particularly after modernization programs began in the 1940s.

Prior to this time, Southern's steam locomotive fleet was a collection of virtually obsolete World War I-era machines built to U.S. Railroad Administration patterns of the early 1920s. Southern's management opted for diesel power in the early 1940s, but wartime shortages of equipment made it difficult to obtain new power. Thus the Southern began an extensive upgrading of its ancient steam locomotives.

These improvements included feedwater heaters (a device that used exhaust steam to heat water before going to the boiler), mechanical stokers, rebuilt cabs, enlarged tenders, single-guide, multiple-bearing cross-heads, mechanical lubricators, low-water alarms, and other smaller devices.

Spencer Shops engines were marked with a look of "tall shoulders." They were equipped with tall ladders on the front of the engines. This modification raised the front part of the running boards even with the middle section of running board (a thin platform suspended above the locomotive valve gear and driver wheels to allow crew and shop workers access to the top of the engine). Often the total number of running boards was reduced from four or five levels to two or three. Besides creating an aesthetic appearance of power, this practical change left more space for servicing the cylinders of the running gear.

The following arrangements were characteristic of Spencer engines from 1940 to the end of steam in 1953:

Tall valve ladders set about 60 degrees from horizontal and joined at the bottom to the front of the pilot beam.

Skewed handrails on the valve ladders. These handrails were typically round and spacious at the top and narrow at the bottom.

A cylindrical headlight with a long finger-nail-shaped visor set just below the center of the boiler.

A bell mounted at the top of the smokebox front on an angle bracket.

Air brake piping on the right side just under the outer edge of the running board from the cab to the front of the engine.

A mechanical lubricator on the right side of the engine, above the valve rod crosshead casting.

A whistle cord over the steam dome and boiler top going into the cab on the right side. Whistle mounted on the steam dome at 25 to 45 degrees forward.

Shallow, welded cab shades.

Raised coal bunker sides.

At the bottom of the cab, narrow walking platforms extending outward, including steps attached to the running boards.

White trim work including sides of the running boards, platform under the smokebox, bottom edge of the pilot, bottom of the cab and tender frame, and wheel tires.

Overall Spencer engines appeared graceful and balanced. Every twist and turn of piping had a purpose. These locomotives thus became a form of architecture in motion.

David Driscoll/SRHA collection

August 1947 view from the coaling tower area looking back at the ready tracks. Note the wheel balancing shed on the right and near it the tank for cleaning solutions used to degrease locomotives.

Spencer railroaders were proud of their hard work and good pay. To maintain their status the workers formed vigorous labor unions

Trade Unions and Strikes

8

Trade unions and union membership played an important role in the lives of Spencer workers. Union membership helped form their individual identities as much as did being railroaders. Unions offered fraternity, security, and solidarity in the workplace and community. Labor Day parades drew thousands to Spencer in the first half of the century, and floats of high school sports teams, churches, and community organizations inched proudly past waving crowds. But the most popular and elaborate floats represented rail unions.

The key role of unions at Spencer Shops was somewhat unusual in the region. The South had been (and remains) recognized for its lack of union activity. Railroaders, however, were an exception. Two of the earliest railroad shop craft unions, for boilermakers and machinists respectively, began in 1888 at Atlanta and quickly spread across the South.

By 1900 almost all transportation and shop craft unions had been absorbed into the American Federation of Labor, a large national craft organization. Various types of trainmen (engineers, firemen, brakemen, and conductors) had separate unions within the AFL as did the individual shop crafts. Spencer was a closed shop, and only union members were allowed to work there in certain crafts.

All the national rail unions had local units at Spencer. Shop clerks were members of locals as were helpers, laborers, and even workers at the transfer sheds. The locals held meetings and social functions, negotiated with management, and organized strikes if necessary. The unions pro-

vided a social function similar to that of Spencer's popular fraternal organizations, the Moose and Masonic lodges. Most unions also had ladies' auxiliaries, much needed social outlets for railroad wives.

Each union kept seniority lists of its members. The workers were listed strictly in order of their hiring by the railroad. A man hired a few days or even a few hours after another in the same craft would be behind that man for his entire career, with quality of work or loyalty to the company playing no part in seniority. A man could move up on the list only if a man ahead of him retired, was fired, or relocated. The unions published small books of seniority lists, which were practically memorized by employees.

The lists were so important because they helped determine who filled job openings in a process called "bidding." When a job became available, a foreman posted a notice on a bulletin board. For much of the steam era Spencer was part of Southern's Danville division. Vacancies at any point in the division were posted at Spencer and all other points so that everyone in the division had a chance at them. An employee bid on a job by writing his name and its title on a piece of paper and depositing it in a box near the bulletin board. After six days the individual bids were turned over to the master mechanic (if the job was in the shops) or the yard master (for jobs in the yard or on train crews).

According to agreements between the unions and the railroad, management had to award the position to the bidder highest on the seniority list of the appropriate craft. Naturally, the highest men could not bid for every

position, and men low on the list often submitted bids in hopes that those ahead of them were satisfied in their current jobs.

When deciding whether to bid for a job, a man considered its location, the pay rate, the hours and shifts he would have to work, and the men he would work with. A man would not bid for a job working with men he could not get along with, even if it offered higher pay. Many men would not bid for a job on the third shift (11:15 p.m. to 7:15 a.m.) because they knew that working all night and sleeping during the day would leave them little family time.

If a man felt that management had been unfair to him in the bidding and hiring process, his local union representative would review the situation and request a meeting with company representatives. If the union agent was still unsatisfied after the meeting, he could appeal the case to the Federal Railroad Labor Board in Washington. While such instances were rare at Spencer, they indicated the important role unions played in employee-management relations. Workers also demanded meetings between management and union representatives if they felt they had been fired unjustly, told to work outside their jurisdiction, or had disagreements about pay or hours. One retired craftsman recalls a busy period in the 1940s when a foreman asked him to work overtime for two consecutive shifts. His second overtime shift ended just as his normal eight-hour shift was beginning. Though he had been on the job for 24 hours, the man did not feel tired and asked to stay on and work his normal shift. The foreman, afraid the man would fall asleep

North Carolina Division of Archives and History

Labor unions enable workers to band together and obtain strength through numbers. Heavily union-ized Spencer workers also commonly posed for group photos.

SENIORITY LIST OF EMPLOYEES REPRESENTED BY THE INTERNATIONAL BROTHERHOOD OF F&O SHOP LABORERS SPENCER, N.C. AS OF JANUARY 1, 1974.		
J. M. Moore	(W)	7-1-26
A. M. Coleman	(S)	4-1-29
W. Mack	(W)	11-14-29
E. Brown	(W)	12-4-29
O. Connor	(W)	4-25-35
L. Moser	(W)	9-8-40
J. R. Ellis	(W)	10-17-40
R. D. Kirk	(W)	11-4-40
B. E. Sims	(W)	5-21-41
G. M. Boler	(TO)	7-16-41
E. W. Williams	(W)	8-20-41
J. Davis	(W)	6-10-42
W. B. McCullough	(W)	9-30-42
J. H. Brown	(F)	10-1-42
L. F. Pitts	(TO)	10-10-42
J. O. Smith	(F)	12-8-42
S. J. Harrison	(F)	1-1-43
J. G. Alexandria	(F)	1-6-43
G. D. Stout	(F)	1-1 5-43
R. L. Sturgis	(F)	2-19-43
A. Holt	(TO)	4-5-43
J. O. Foster	(F)	11-23-43
C. H. Hawkins	(F)	12-1-43
M. R. Wood	(F)	4-20-44
R. Chambers	(F)	5-22-44
F. M. McCullough	(TO)	8-1-44
I. Bost	(F)	8-21-44
W. Peeler	(F)	11-1-44
P. Hardin	(F)	1-29-45
W. O. Ellis	(F)	4-2-45
R. E. Washington	(W)	4-5-45
J. P. Henderson	(W)	7-7-45
R. J. Hill	(F)	10-31-45
J. E. Seiler	(F)	11-3-45
J. Hobson	(F)	11-6-45
C. Snow	(F)	11-14-45
J. E. Jamison	(TO)	2-12-47
F. H. Guyton	(F)	8-5-47
D. P. Conyers	(F)	8-11-47
M. A. Hoover	(F)	3-16-48
E. Tillman	(F)	3-17-48
W. Boler	(F)	7-27-48
A. J. Henderson	(F)	9-20-50
A. Davis	(F)	12-22-50
W. Perry	(F)	1-23-51

North Carolina Division of Archives and History

Seniority was crucial in determining who got the best union jobs. This 1974 list reveals men with almost 50 years of seniority.

at his job, sternly refused. The man called his union representative, a craftsman on that shift, to help argue his case. Threatened with having the issue taken to higher authority, the foreman gave in but told the crafts-man that for safety he should just sit in a chair and do nothing for the whole shift. This suited him just fine.

The most dramatic incidents related to unions at Spencer were strikes. Strikes were infrequent but disrupted both shop operations and workers' lives. On May 30, 1901, just five years after Spencer Shops opened, machinists struck at the shops of Southern and other railroads across the United States. The machinists' national union had sent a list of demands to railroad executives for a reduction of working hours from ten to nine per day without a drop in wages, limits on the number of apprentices, and changes in rules for overtime. When company executives offered only further talks, the machin-ists walked off their jobs. The strike became national in scope and includ-ed machinists in other industries.

Southern worked quickly to replace the striking machinists with strikebreakers from outside the area

and non-union local machinists. The strikers diligently picketed the shops and kept an eye out for arriving strike-breakers. The *Salisbury Daily Sun* for June 13 reported that four machinists had been smuggled into the shops by train the night before. The men were in a darkened car and were not dis-covered until the train was pulling out.

The railway hired guards to pro-tect the strikebreakers, but there were no reported incidents of violence at the shops proper. One strikebreaker was attacked by several men when he left town on a train to visit his family in Asheville. Bystanders helped him fend off the attackers, but their iden-tities were not confirmed, and no arrests were made.

On July 25, two months after the strike began, Southern president Samuel Spencer stated that further negotiations with strikers were not necessary as the company was success-fully replacing them. The strikers' resolve weakened and many asked for their jobs back. Most were denied this as the company decided its replace-ment machinists would become per-manent employees. The *Daily Sun* concluded that the strike "failed to

accomplish much for those who par-ticipated, but . . . succeeded only in inconveniencing many persons in many other lines of business through-out the country."

Other major confrontations came after World War I, during which fed-eral control of the railroads had increased bargaining power for the unions. Workers gained other conces-sions, including wage hikes and reduced hours, but the recession and high inflation after the war negated wage increases.

In the summer of 1919 rail employees began talking of strikes. In late July rail unions held a series of meetings with the U.S. Railroad Administration (the USRA still con-trolled the railroads as it had during the war), but the workers grew impa-tient. On July 31 over 60,000 railroad-ers walked off their jobs in impromp-tu and loosely organized strikes.

On August 4 union locals at Spencer joined the strike. Over 1500 men struck at Spencer including helpers, laborers, and all foremen. It was the first time that the huge shop complex had been shut down, and the men hoped it would not be long before the government heeded their demand for higher wages. President Woodrow Wilson called on shopmen across the nation to return to work and allow normal negotiations to carry through. On August 11, after only a week, Spencer shopmen grudgingly agreed to go back to work, as did most other strikers across the country. A few weeks later the USRA agreed to raise wages over the next year. Because it lasted only eight days, the strike caused no great disruption, but it foreshadowed a greater drama soon to come.

The government ran the railroads for 26 months and granted wage increases (to offset wartime inflation) and more bargaining power for unions. In 1920 Congress passed the Esch-Cummings (or Transportation) Act, ending federal control. The government feared that private companies, when back in control, would try to reverse the gains labor had made under the USRA, and there would be more trouble with the unions. To mediate disputes between management and labor, Congress created the Railroad Labor Board, a body made up of government officials, union representatives, and railroad executives. As expected, the companies started cutting wages and benefits, and several cases came before the board. It often decided in favor of the companies, who promised they would be forced into bankruptcy if they did not cut wages. Shop unions in particular were dismayed with the rulings and felt they were carrying a greater burden of the cuts.

On June 6, 1922, the board ruled that shop crafts must accept yet another 7 to 9 cent-per-hour decrease in wages. Representatives of shop unions then voted unanimously for a national strike to begin July 1. Spencer shopmen accepted the call to strike. All craftsmen and most helpers and foremen laid down their tools and took up picket signs. None knew this would not be "just another strike." Strikers

SALISb

SALISBU

VOL. XVII—NO. 25

STRIKE TALK AT SPENCER SHOPS

Men, Forced to Work in Cold Round House, Carry Matter to President Spencer at Washington.

COMMITTEE OF EMPLOYEES WENT THERE LAST NIGHT

Fires in Stoves Put Out Last Friday to Cut Expenses and Discontent, Already Existing, Comes to a Head.

North Carolina Division of Archives and History
Major labor problems at Spencer, such as a potential strike in 1905, were headline news in local papers.

manned picket lines in shifts, watching for replacements which Southern might send to the shops. Southern did not hire strikebreakers in the first weeks of the strike and kept trains running surprisingly well using only the labor of high-ranking foremen and even master mechanics. Conferences between rail and union officials stalemated, and the strike became an endurance test.

On July 17 Governor Cameron Morrison, concerned over violence by strikers in other parts of the nation, ordered National Guard troops to Raleigh, Durham, Rocky Mount, and Hamlet to prevent possible violence by striking shopmen on the Seaboard Air Line and Atlantic Coast Line railroads. The governor did not send troops to Spencer at that point, but the town was not immune to strike-related violence. On August 15 Southern president Fairfax Harrison announced that he would hire workers to replace strikers. Pickets at Spencer began an around-the-clock vigil at the shops. Nearly 500 strikers on each shift covered all entrances to the 150-acre site. Some blacks employed as helpers since the strike began quietly left the shops the night of August 11 to visit their families, but they were discovered and beaten severely by white strikers. The names of the assailants were not reported, and no arrests were made.

On August 18 forty strikebreakers arrived by train. They were escorted into the shops by Rowan County sheriff J. H. Krider under the glaring eyes of picketing strikers who carried "sticks of large, walking cane size." Krider saw enough glaring to request National Guard troops. Governor Morrison hesitated because no large-scale violence had occurred but, after a call from Southern vice president Henry Miller, sent 500 troops to Salisbury on August 20. The Guardsmen pitched their tents three miles from Spencer at the Rowan County fairgrounds, which they dubbed "Camp Morrison."

Within a week of Harrison's decision to hire strikebreakers, over 300 were sent piecemeal to Spencer from other parts of the country. Leaders at the shops felt it would be unsafe for scabs to walk back and forth to local boarding houses, so the men had to

PRICE: FIVE CENT

WATER SUPPLY TO SHOPS AT SPENCER CUT OFF BY EXPLOSION OF DYNAMITE

stay in the shop buildings

Promiscuous Early Morning Firing and Burning of Several Box Cars Serve To Heighten Excitement.

NO TROOPS ORDERED FOR GUARD DUTY AT SHOPS BY COL. SCOTT

Explosion Blows Out Section of Twelve-Inch Main Feeding W... The

24 hours a day. The complex thus became a community within itself as the railway provided food and clothing for the confined strikebreakers. Witnesses claimed that large amounts of illegal alcohol were used to help the strikebreakers endure the boredom of life at the shops. Once a week a non-striking foremen drove his car through the picket lines, the strikers never realizing that his trunk held the county's finest bootlegged whiskey.

On the night of August 20 a dynamite explosion severed the main water pipeline to the shops and an idle boxcar on the perimeter of the site mysteriously caught fire, causing great excitement in Spencer and Salisbury. Southern officials tried to pin the blame on strikers who in turn said the explosion was an "inside job" meant to turn local residents against them.

The next day Methodist minister Tom Jamison of Spencer, a supporter of the strikers, was attacked in downtown Salisbury by John Sloop, a postal clerk who felt the strike was damaging the community. A gathering crowd threatened Sloop before he was taken into protective custody by Sheriff Krider.

The excitement was enough for the commander of the National Guard troops to send five companies of men to the shops that evening. Firemen, engineers, conductors, and brakemen based at Spencer thought that the commander had overreacted by sending troops and began a sympathy strike to support the shopmen. They refused to move trains out of the Spencer yard the next morning, which almost completely shut down operations at the site. R. E. Simpson, Southern's general superintendent for the district, saw disaster looming if trains could not move and hastily requested that the troops be withdrawn. They went back to Camp Morrison after having been at the shops less than 12 hours. The trainmen promptly returned to work.

A small contingent of troops remained at the Salisbury post office to protect Sloop, who had been

North Carolina Division of Archives and History

Machines such as this quartering machine were idle at Spencer Shops during the great strike of 1922 unless operated by management or strikebreakers.

ALL TRAFFIC ON SOUTHERN TIED UP WHEN TRAINMEN WALK OUT IN PROTEST AGAINST ARMED GUARDS

CALL FOR TROOPS FOLLOWS ATTACK

Five Companies Of Militia Take Charge At Spencer

Unless Brotherhood Men, Switchmen and Clerks at Spencer Reverse Action Tie-up Will Be Complete

released from jail. This was a wise decision as the strikers were showing less inclination to remain peaceful. On the night of August 21 nine black strikebreakers from Winston-Salem who had been allowed outside the shop area were seized in Salisbury by at least 24 masked men. The men took the frightened strikebreakers across the Yadkin River, less than five miles from Spencer, and told them to start running. One ran too slowly to suit his assailants and was shot in the leg. A passerby spotted the injured man and reported the incident to Sheriff Krider, who took him to the Salisbury hospital. The fact that all the black men were scabs led Krider to suspect the striking shopmen, but the assailants were never identified.

The strike continued without incident thereafter, and the governor removed the troops on August 31. By this time the strike had been underway for two months, and the strikers were tiring. Newspapers reported that picket stations were often deserted.

Meanwhile union, railroad, and government representatives parlayed almost continuously with no results. President Warren G. Harding personally met with both sides for several weeks. No plan was worked out because the railroads insisted that strikebreakers be retained and included on seniority lists, an idea unacceptable to the unions.

On September 8 the national chairmen of the shop crafts began urging strikers to seek separate settlements with their respective companies. Within a week strikers on 11 railroads agreed to return to work at the reduced wages established by the Railroad Labor Board back in June. On September 18 Southern and its shop workers reached a settlement: all strikers could return to work at "present rates of pay" unless they had been guilty of violence during the strike. A commission of six union and six company representatives would settle questions of seniority lists and attempt to determine who had been responsible for violent acts.

After the national strike the shop unions were battered and weak. Some railroads had filled their shops with replacement workers whom they organized in "company unions," which had no connections with the American Federation of Labor and could not be drawn into another national strike. Of major railroads in the South, only Southern and the Seaboard Air Line recognized the independent, national unions after the strike. Given this, shopmen at Spencer were lucky just to be able to return to their jobs. On July 23, 1923, most Southern shopmen finally got a raise—two cents an hour.

In Spencer the bitterness of the strike did not die quickly. Some enmity had developed between striking shopmen and trainmen who, except for the day the National Guardsmen came to the shops, never joined the strike. The trainmen passed daily through picket lines manned by their friends and neighbors. The few shopmen who had not struck faced even greater derision. The extent to which the bitter feelings endured is uncertain, although one Spencer resident born soon after the strike claims that scabs were remembered as such for decades. Only the Great Depression brought the community back together—against a threat far greater than any strike.

The 1922 strike was the longest and most bitter labor dispute at Spencer. In subsequent years the influence of the unions declined steadily, angering shopmen who felt that in return for their loyalty the unions should remain strong. Later, when massive layoffs swept the entire industry in the diesel era, the unions were weakest when labor needed them most.

Ties *magazine*

It was not uncommon for several members of one family to work at the Shops. Here E. M. Cauble and his son, M. R. Cauble, service a diesel locomotive axle using a device invented by the son.

The Daily Grind

9

Most Spencer shopmen worked one of three eight-hour shifts. The shifts began at 7:15 a.m. and 3:15 and 11:15 p.m. For years after the shops opened in 1896, men often worked 12 or 16-hour shifts. Government regulations and union-company agreements eventually led to an eight-hour workday, the standard for most years the shops were in operation. The roundhouse, switching yard, and car repair shed operated every day of the year on three shifts. Other buildings, including the back shop, had first and second shifts only and occasionally shut down on weekends and holidays.

At each shift change a local "shop train" arrived at the site to unload workers from Salisbury. It soon filled up with workers just finishing their shift, ready for the 15-minute return trip to Salisbury. On several occasions as the train left the shops, it was followed by a hapless apprentice running to catch it while pulling up the straps of his overalls or tugging a coat over his work clothes. Other workers arrived by car or, in early years, horse-drawn wagon. Many more lived close enough to walk.

Roundhouse workers often gathered near the building for several minutes before their shift began to "shoot the breeze." Most also went to the locker room to change clothes. One got very dirty in almost any non-clerical job at the shops, so each craftsman kept a set of work clothes in his locker.

As the shift change approached, men lined up near the roundhouse ticket office to "clock on." In the early years they signed a card, but electric punch clocks were installed later. As the craftsmen clocked on, a foreman handed them tickets listing the repair projects to tackle first. Craftsmen tried to finish each assignment before their shifts ended, but if one was in the middle of a job at shift change, a man on the next shift finished it. Unless a particular locomotive needed to be put back in service immediately no standard time was allotted for its repair.

The workday in the back shop was similar to that in the roundhouse. Before clocking on, back shop craftsmen changed in locker rooms at each end of the building. Some jobs kept men in a certain part of the machine shop or in a specialty shop in the gallery for almost their entire shift. Others worked on locomotives in the erecting shop which were in various stages of overhaul. Usually a man worked on one locomotive until he finished his assigned tasks, then moved to another. Since the locomotives did not move by in assembly line fashion, he had to move his tools every time he worked on a different locomotive. As his seniority increased and tasks became more specialized, his collection of tools grew. The tool-

David Driscoll/SRHA collection

Hat in hand and goggles around his neck, W. R. Weant posed with engine No. 1210 on Sept. 15, 1946, in the roundhouse.

Life was not all humdrum routine at Spencer. Shopmen designed and created Southern's only streamlined steam locomotive, The Tennessean, shown here in 1947.

boxes of oldtimers often evolved into elaborate tool carts pushed around by helpers. Craftsmen made many of their tools by hand and put considerable time into producing personal toolboxes. The most pernicious prank a worker could pull was to hide another's tools, especially if he was in the middle of a job with a deadline.

Most men in the back shop worked the first shift. The few on the second shift generally did non-specialized tasks such as stripping parts off locomotives or moving them around the erecting shop with the two large cranes. Thus men on the first shift could stop tasks when their shift ended and come in the next morning to finish them expecting that their work area would be undisturbed.

The men had breaks during each workday, but the lunch break was the most eagerly anticipated. Krider's Cafe, which opened across from the shops on Salisbury Avenue in 1943, was a popular destination for railroaders because of its location and reputation for good food. Owner Evelyn Krider sent a menu over to the shops so the men could order ahead of time. They only had about 15 minutes to eat after cleaning up and walking to the restaurant, so they plunged into Krider's "like a herd of cows," as one retiree recalls. "You dared not get their seats," adds Mrs. Krider. "They gener-

ally liked something that would stick to them, pinto beans and dumplings, chicken-fried steak. No fancy vegetables like broccoli."

Many other shopmen ate at the YMCA or the boarding houses in Spencer and East Spencer which served meals to the public. Others brought lunch from home or had it delivered by a dutiful wife or child. Spencer children relished the opportunity to take Dad his lunch. Although they could not go in, it offered an opportunity at least to get close to the loud, mysterious, smoking shop buildings. On sunny days or clear nights some shopmen climbed ladders to the tops of buildings and ate looking out over the shops and town. They watched children delivering lunches or playing in the town park. They knew that for many boys the daily grind of shop work would become reality only too soon.

Company policy stipulated that each worker wait until five minutes before shift change to begin cleaning his tools and work area, but many stopped earlier if they were not especially busy. After cleaning up their work area, men walked to the locker rooms to wash and change clothes, then clocked off and went home. Yet most workers relished the opportunity to stay on and work overtime which paid time and a half for each hour

over eight on any regular day and all day on Sundays and holidays.

For some master craftsmen, shop work offered opportunities for creativity and variety. For most workers, however, it was simply dirty and tedious. Occasionally they broke the monotony with pranks upon fellow workers. Retired shopmen never run short of stories about pranks but usually withhold names to protect the guilty. One story concerns lunch boxes which workers kept on benches in the locker room. After each shift they hurried by to scoop up the boxes on the way to the shop train or an auto. One day someone nailed a man's lunch box to the bench. When he ran by to grab his box, he picked up the entire bench, spilling all the boxes on the floor and causing a flurry of laughter and cursing. The locker room was the scene of numerous pranks; many a startled worker opened his locker after a long workday to find a live opossum staring at him.

Men easily frightened often were victims of pranks. One dark night a skittish laborer, who aligned the turntable and guided locomotives into the roundhouse, received special treatment. Someone made a human-like dummy, covered it with a red substance resembling blood, and put it on the front of a locomotive going to the roundhouse. Seeing the dummy, the laborer screamed and scrambled to the roundhouse office, returning with a foreman who quickly discovered the ruse. The foreman never identified the culprits, but he need only have followed the sound of laughter.

It was difficult to pull pranks in the back shop because of its many workers and constant activity. Yet certain apprentices took pleasure in pouring liquids from the balcony of the machine shop onto the main floor below. Most popular were oil and water. Each caused great consternation and cursing if poured on an operating machine. Apprentices fled hurriedly after such incidents to avoid capture and reprimand.

Pranks were not the only extracurricular activities on the shop floors. Craftsmen fashioned personal items from scrap metal, a common practice in railroad shops. Men produced numerous frying pans in the back shop as well as farm tools and other kitchen utensils. One man made a swing set for his children, while another crafted a ring for his wife from locomotive parts. Foremen allowed such prohibited activity on a limited basis.

Pranks and frivolity were part of the work experience at Spencer but did not interfere with quality of work or safety. Day-to-day activity at Spencer had enough potentially dangerous circumstances to keep men on their toes. Moving parts were a great danger, especially when leather belts connected machine tools to their motors. In the machine shop these heavy belts often stretched 20 feet off the floor to motors attached to roof supports. Human limbs and clothing were easily caught in the uncovered belts, and a person might be carried to the ceiling then thrown violently back down.

Rapidly spinning machines and metal shavings sprayed from parts being machined were another hazard. Machine operators wore goggles and followed strict safety procedures. Workmen using welders and metal cutters in the boiler shop had to guard against fire causing stray sparks. While most buildings contained little or no structural wood, fire and explosions were a threat because of the wood-brick flooring in some buildings and the presence of large oil and fuel storage facilities. Bright light from electric arc welding was also dangerous to eyes.

The ubiquitous tracks in the freight yard were a hazard for derelicts and careless employees who were occasionally hit at night by passing

The Tennessean sported clean streamlining on its front end and, on one trip, Duke and Georgia Tech pennants.

trains. Anyone foolish enough to pass between the cars of a train being assembled could be crushed between them. Falls into pits or from locomotives and rail cars occurred in the yard or shops when hurrying workers neglected safety procedures.

Both labor and management at Spencer worked hard for safety. If an injury was not clearly caused by negligence, changes in procedures or work environment usually were made. Safety committees with representatives of both labor and management suggested physical changes or modifications in procedures to improve safety. Committee members offering safety suggestions might receive letters of thanks from Southern officials, but there was no guarantee ideas would be used.

Southern sponsored safety contests on departmental, site, and system-wide levels. A contest at the Spencer storehouse in 1947 was typical. Stores department employees divided into two teams, "reds" and "blues," to earn points for safety activities: five points for each pair of safety shoes sold, one point for each unsafe

Pranks and fun on Southern were not limited to Spencer Shops. Here milepost 57 is adorned to celebrate the 57th birthday of general manager R. E. Simpson.

condition or fire hazard corrected, and 20 points for a safety suggestion which the company implemented at all storehouses. Ten points were deducted for each severe accident, five for a minor accident with time lost, and one for a minor accident with no time lost. After a fierce but friendly competition, the blues won (by selling more shoes) and were treated to dinner by the reds. Similar contests were held between shops in a division and between divisions within the Southern system. *Ties*, the company magazine, listed which of the three geographic divisions in the system had the best monthly safety records. Many trophies still kept today at the

museum attest to Spencer's success in safety contests.

The shops had many warning and safety devices to combat potentially dangerous situations. Signs warning of hazards or listing safety procedures step-by-step were a common sight. Safety slogan contests were held periodically with winning entries placed on signs throughout the shops.

Despite all precautions many accidents did occur, some so severe that they passed into local legend and lore. Perhaps the most spectacular accident took place on Thursday, October 1, 1908. At about 5:40 p.m. workers noticed a caboose on a side track near the powder house had

caught fire. The powder house was a small metal building near the blacksmith shop filled with gunpowder, dynamite, railroad torpedoes, and fuses. Someone quickly turned in an alarm.

The shops had an elaborate firefighting system with workers on every shift trained to operate fire equipment. The horn which sounded the alarm was in the powerhouse. A certain number of blasts signaled a fire, and members of the fire brigade would immediately drop what they were doing and hurry to the location of the fire, also given by horn signals. The fire brigade transported water hoses on reel carts. Hauling the hoses

On Oct. 14, 1945, as goat No. 1575 swung around on the turntable, it struck diesel No. 4307 parked nearby. The goat, with engine No. 1479, hung over the end of the turntable, derailing four drivers.

and connecting them to hydrants required such skill that fire teams across the nation competed in timed hose reel races (described below).

The caboose caught fire during shift change, however, and there were few people at the site to form an effective fire brigade. Three men managed to connect a hose and begin dousing the caboose with water. Charles Leyton, a flue maker at the roundhouse, and his helper George Gould ran to the powder house to do what they could to help. Another employee, John Crowell, also rushed to the scene. As he approached the fire, Crowell saw smoke rising from the powder house. Apparently sparks from the burning caboose had fallen on the building's roof. As Crowell turned to run, the contents of the powder house exploded with a sound that shook buildings many miles away. Crowell was thrown several feet through the air, receiving cuts and bruises on his face when he landed. He was one of the lucky ones. Leyton and Gould were nearest the powder house when it exploded, and both died soon after. Two other men, James T. Goble and Fletcher Stafford, had been standing together not far from the powder house. After the explosion they were

found 400 feet apart, both seriously injured. Over 20 workers received injuries in the blast. Southern's local medical staff was summoned from the Spencer YMCA. Goble, Stafford, and several others were taken to the hospital. Goble died that night, but all the others eventually recovered.

Besides destroying the powder house and one end of the blacksmith shop, the blast blew out nearly every window in nearby shop buildings and many windows along Salisbury Avenue in Spencer. Property damage at the shops alone reached hundreds of thousands of dollars. The railway investigated for several days but concluded only that spontaneous combustion had caused the fire. Management learned a lesson: subsequent powder houses sat alone at the extreme northern end of the shops.

An injury enduring in Spencer lore occurred in March 1911 to a young boilermaker apprentice. The man had worked overtime on his first day and was eager to catch a departing shop train when he finally got off. In haste he ran through a wall of vapor rising from the ground. He had no idea the vapor was coming from an open lye pit used to wash grease and oil off locomotive parts. Lye, an excellent cleaner of metal, is also very caustic to human skin. The apprentice ran through the vapor and fell into the pit over his head. When rescuers pulled him out, he left most of his skin behind. He was still alive but in such pain that he begged them to kill him. They refused, opened a clean bale of cotton for him to lay in, and poured oil over his body while waiting for an ambulance. The man died at the hospital several hours later. The lye pit was subsequently moved, but the story was told to new apprentices as a lesson in the dangers at the shops.

Accidents of such magnitude were rare. Despite the dangers inherent in shopwork, a man could avoid serious injury by always being atten-

OBER 7, 1908.

A FATAL EXPLOSION

Powder House Blown Up at Spencer, N. C. Shops

TWO DEAD; SEVERAL INJURED

Two Men Killed and Many Others Injured Thursday Afternoon by Blow-Up of Powder House at Southern Shops—Buildings Wrecked and Much Property Destroyed.

Spencer, N. C., Special.—Two men killed outright, two so badly hurt that they can hardly recover and fifteen or more slightly injured, with a destruction of thousands of dollars' worth of property, is the result of a terrible blow-up Thursday afternoon of the house in which the Southern Railway Company kept stored its powder and other explosives used in connection with the work at its large shops here. The plant is badly wrecked and work is at a standstill for some time.

The dead are Charlie Leyton, an unmarried man about 45 years of age, whose body was mangled and charred almost beyond recognition and George Gould, colored.

Those believed to be fatally injured are:

Fletcher Stafford and James T. Gobbel.

Those slightly injured are:

Kaderly, master mechani-

The Spencer Crescent reported the disastrous explosion at the powder house in October 1908.

Hundreds of constantly shifting cars in the freight yard posed a danger to workers and anyone careless enough to pass between them.

tive to his work and surroundings. It was difficult to avoid other unpleasant aspects of shopwork, however. The most conspicuous characteristic of work at the shops was filth. Dirt, dust, grease, oil, soot, and smoke from locomotives inundated the buildings. Noise, from machines and locomotives, was also a problem. Most buildings were very hot in summer and very cold in winter. Those whose jobs kept them outside, such as locomotive cleaners and wipers and coal, water, and sand loaders, worked their shifts no matter the weather. Workers' comfort was not a primary concern at the shops.

The shopmen were compensated by higher wages and greater benefits than in other industries. Their jobs also gave them privileged status in the community. Even Rowan County natives with successful careers in business and politics admitted to being jealous of the railroaders. The romantic aura surrounding railroads captured Americans of all ages. To children who stared wide-eyed at trains as

they rumbled by, engineers and other crewmen were cavaliers of the rails. Shopmen who kept the trains running, while less recognizable, enjoyed elevated status by simple association. In Spencer adults found themselves adjusting crossheads or dropping wheels on locomotives they had come to love as children. "There's a romance that goes along with the steam engine that you never get over once you've worked with them," admits retired electrician John Dry. "You get the feeling after you've worked with them that they're a living thing." For most shopmen the chance to be "workin' for the railroad" was its own compensation.

It was in Southern's interest to keep workers satisfied and help them cope with job pressures. The company sponsored popular diversions to provide entertainment and develop a sense of community among workers. For several years after the shops opened, the railroad held picnics in which shopworkers, trainmen, and families rode special trains to places

such as Winston-Salem and Danville, Virginia, for a day of fun, games, and, above all, eating.

Another diversion involved hose reel races, which were popular throughout the country before World War I. Men on reel teams pulled the hose reel carts used by fire departments before the spread of motorized vehicles. The carts were supported by two large wooden wheels. Long bars stuck out from each cart by which it could be pulled. A water hose was rolled up on a reel between the wheels. All large industrial complexes kept reel carts for use by firefighting teams. Many city fire departments also used hose reels around 1900, although horses replaced men if carts had to cover a long distance.

Speed and efficiency were essential in operating hose reels. Teams practiced many hours to perform quickly and without error. The idea developed to have competing reel teams. Competition teams, organized at Spencer Shops by 1899, quickly developed a reputation for quality.

At contests, eight-man reel teams raced against a clock, not head-to-head against other teams. When the race began, the men ran a short distance to the reel and pulled it to a hydrant. A man hooked one end of the hose to the hydrant, and the team pulled the reel ahead until the hose was completely unrolled, usually 100 to 150 yards. Then a "nozzle-man," who ran beside the team carrying the nozzle, screwed it onto the other end of the hose. The man at the hydrant turned on the water, and timing ended when it came out of the nozzle. The shortest time won the race.

When the Spencer team traveled to official competitions, the railway paid expenses and granted members vacation pay. The team kept the prize money that it won, and it won often. In 1904 the team set a world record in St. Louis, completing the race and "showing water" at the end of the nozzle in 24 1/5 seconds. The 1909 team lowered the record time to 23 3/5 seconds in Asheville. Spencer teams performed well throughout the twenties, collecting more world and state championship titles.

As in other sports where the fate of the whole team often rests on the skill of one or two members, the men of the Spencer reel teams became close friends. Each had won his position in tryouts in which all white shopmen were invited to participate, so members carried the notion that they were the best and fastest runners in the community. They gave each other nicknames and, despite company rules, drank together while traveling to competitions.

The teams practiced on Fifth Street in Spencer. Practice was crucial to avoid errors. If a nozzle on a hydrant was not screwed on properly, it would blow off when the water pressure was turned on, disqualifying the team and creating a hazard for those nearby. The Spencer team lost one race in 1909 at Asheville when a

North Carolina Division of Archives and History

Spencer Shops fielded a number of championship hose reel teams. One team poses here with their hose reel behind them.

connector was blown loose from a hydrant and struck a member in the ribs, injuring him severely.

The Shops stopped sending teams to competitions during the Great Depression, when the railway could not afford to sponsor many recreational activities. By then the popularity of reel teams had carried over into nearby towns. A team from East Spencer won the world championship in 1928 and 1930. A segregated reel team of black athletes was organized in East Spencer in 1911. The team was dubbed "White Rose reel team number three" and was often champion of a league of black teams. East Spencer even organized a women's reel team in 1933. It was apparently the only one in the area as it competed in the men's division. Exploits of Spencer area teams and others across the state are chronicled in the North Carolina Firemen's Museum in New Bern.

Baseball has always been popular in Spencer, and around 1902 Southern sponsored a semi-pro team of railroaders which played teams from surrounding towns. A ball field was marked off in the town park directly across Salisbury Avenue from the shops. The Spencer team quickly became skilled and won the state

semi-pro championship in 1906, beating a team from Reidsville 6 to 5. Many town folk watched the games, and the Spencer Crescent reported on every contest, both home and away.

For many years the outfield at Spencer was bounded by a canvas fence which was put up and taken down for every game. Local boys performed this task, their pay being free admission to the game. In 1919 supporters of the team decided to erect a permanent metal fence. The eight-foot-high fence was constructed and installed by boilermakers and machinists from the shops. To help pay for the metal, citizens of Spencer invited two major league teams to play an exhibition game there after spring training in Florida. The Detroit Tigers and Boston Braves (later of Milwaukee and Atlanta) agreed to play on March 30, 1920. Over 6,000 people showed up at the park on game day. Most of them came to catch a glimpse of Detroit's Ty Cobb, probably the best known player in the country at the time. The "Georgia Peach" decided not to show up, however, and stayed in his Salisbury hotel room, much to the chagrin of fans at Spencer. The Braves defeated the Cobb-less Tigers 7 to 6.

On train crews African Americans were not allowed to be engineers. Here are two black train crewmen, a fireman and perhaps a brakeman, on locomotive No. 1722 at Salisbury.

Women and Minorities at the Shops

Diversions and recreation helped workers deal with the pressures of their jobs, but some workers faced greater challenges because of their skin color or gender. African Americansalways formed an integral part of the shops community, though they were usually relegated to unskilled positions. The part of Rowan County in which Southern built the shops was populated by many black families. This might have been because a large antebellum plantation, Spring Hill, had been located just east of the shops site. Descendants of former slaves formed a community in this area named "Spring Hill" even after it and the surrounding land were incorporated as East Spencer in 1901. The majority of the land on which the shops were built had been owned by a black farmer named Robert Partee before John S. Henderson purchased it for the railroad.

Teams of black laborers helped build the shops in 1896. When regular operation began, the railway hired many blacks as laborers and helpers. Helpers assisted craftsmen with physical labor, but unions and railroads disapproved of African-American helpers becoming craftsmen themselves. They thus remained helpers for their entire careers and earned a great deal of seniority. African Americans usually topped helper seniority lists (which included whites) and could bid for the favored jobs. "Favored" often meant highest paying, as helper jobs had different pay scales according to their complexity or physical danger. For example, helpers at the tremendous "heavy fire" forges in the blacksmith shop endured intense heat and physical exertion but earned more than other helpers. Black helpers at Southern finally were allowed to apprentice to become craftsmen in the late 1960s, but by then Spencer Shops had closed. Some blacks, transferred to other shops after the closing, eventually became craftsmen and foremen.

Black laborers kept the buildings and shop grounds free of debris. During the steam era many were wipers who kept locomotives cleaned and shined. African-American laborers loaded and unloaded supplies in the storehouse, filled locomotives with fuel and water, and shoveled out the cinder pits at the coal chutes. They could ultimately be called upon to do any job deemed necessary by a foreman.

Many African Americans worked on trains as firemen, though for decades they could not be promoted to engineer. Blacks also served on trains as Pullman porters and cooks. A few worked in the yard as brakemen, and some were hostler helpers who operated the turntable at the roundhouse while hostlers pushed locomotives into the stalls with switch engines.

Numerous African Americans labored at the transfer sheds several hundred yards south of the shops. Retirees who worked at the sheds during the 1940s and 1950s claim that most non-managerial positions there were filled by blacks. Some were women who began careers at the sheds during the labor shortages of World War II. Both men and women served as packers and drivers, loading, unloading, and moving freight between boxcars. African

Americans at the transfer sheds were paid less than black shop workers but still earned more than other unskilled laborers in the county.

The ceiling on African-American advancement at Spencer was accompanied by segregated facilities. Water fountains and locker rooms remained segregated through the late 1950s. African-American shop workers who went to a restaurant or boarding house for lunch had to enter through a back door and eat apart from white patrons. Passenger trains had separate cars for blacks and whites. Some individual cars (Jim Crow cars) had separate sections for black and white passengers. Streetcars and buses also had sections for each race. Even unions were segregated, as black and white workers gathered in separate locals with separate treasuries and social functions.

Over the years the town of East Spencer became predominantly black, while Spencer remained almost completely white. In East Spencer segregated schools and churches served each race. As Southern's main line divided Spencer from East Spencer, the black and white children of railroaders literally grew up "across the tracks" from each other.

Despite segregation both African-American and white retirees report that race relations on the shop floor were usually cordial. Most duties required the cooperation of several persons, and if a fellow employee could be counted on, his race was unimportant. "We got along fine," a white retiree recalled, "because it was hard work and each man was supposed to do his job." A black retiree stated further that white craftsmen generally stood up for their African American helpers if they were the objects of racial slurs. Bonds between craftsmen and helpers seem particularly strong, perhaps because they worked side-by-side daily. Interracial friendships built on the job ultimately carried over into private life. Today black and white retirees share lake houses and often fish or do other activities together.

This does not mean there were no racial confrontations on the job, especially when African American strikebreakers were involved. A black helper recalls that during a strike in the 1920s (possibly the great strike of 1922) his father could not come home for several days. He had agreed to remain on the job and was afraid that if he left the shops he would be beaten by white pickets. Overwhelming evidence from interviews with black and white retirees reveals, however, that such incidents were rare. Nearly every employee had an integral role in operation of the shops, and race necessarily played second fiddle to job performance.

The earliest record of a woman working at Spencer is from the *Southern News Bulletin* of February 1921 which noted that "Miss Nellie Richmond" had been working at the Shops since 1917 and was a third-generation railroader. The women who followed her were few in number and held only office jobs (such as stenographer, switchboard operator, timekeeper, and clerk) but played an essential role in daily operations.

Mary Kneeburg of Spencer (and later Salisbury) is an example of a woman who made a career of railroading. In 1929 she began as a clerk in the transfer sheds, checking the rail cars being loaded there for damaged freight. She filled out reports on any damage, filed them, and watched to see that each car was loaded with the correct merchandise. After taking time off to start a family, Kneeburg became a clerk in the master mechanic's office and in the car department where she kept records of freight car repairs. She recalls that only a couple of other women ever worked alongside her. One of those was Frances Phillips, who worked in the master

David Driscoll/SRHA collection

Photographs of African American workers at Spencer are rare. This portrait of laborer G. Miller on Sept. 29, 1946, on the tender of locomotive No. 585 at the roundhouse is one of them.

mechanic's office for 31 years. One of her duties was to write travel passes for Southern employees and families. In this role she became friends with many railroad workers and townspeople. Phillips loved her job and traveled extensively on the discounted employee rates.

Many of the women hired to work at the Spencer transfer sheds during the labor shortages of World War II continued working at the sheds after the war until the facility closed. They recall good treatment by male co-workers and saw the work as a necessity to support their families. Local lore holds that several African-American women worked at the shops as locomotive wipers and washers (jobs normally held by male laborers) during World War I, but no known written evidence reinforces this claim. Retirees remember no other instances of women working in the shops as helpers, laborers, or craftspersons. Retired trainmen do recall that in the mid-1970s, near the time that the Spencer freight yard shut down, women were beginning to train as engineers. Railroading had indeed changed.

Jim Wrinn

In 1939 General Motors produced its revolutionary first road freight diesel, the FT, which proved the diesel's superiority to steam. Here the original FT demonstrator, No. 103, visits Spencer as a traveling museum piece 50 years later.

The Diesel Era

10

The first diesel locomotive arrived at Spencer Shops in 1941—towed in by a steam locomotive. This revolutionary new locomotive was the culmination of a lengthy development fraught with distrust, intrigue, and the mysterious disappearance of its brilliant inventor.

Rudolf Diesel, born in Paris in 1858, returned to his parents' native Germany to study engineering. Like many others in Europe and America, he sought to develop an alternative to the steam engine. Typical steam engines only converted six to eight percent of their produced heat into useful work. Internal combustion engines, developed in the mid 1800s by various German and Belgian scientists, were significantly more efficient. They exploded a mixture of gas and oxygen inside a sealed cylinder and were used in the first automobiles in the 1890s. Diesel sought an even more efficient engine and produced his first working model in 1897.

Earlier internal combustion engines required an electric spark to ignite the air-fuel mixture. Diesel's engine compressed the air in a cylinder, heating it to over 1,000 degrees. At that point a small amount of oil was squirted into the cylinder. It instantly ignited, pushing down a piston in the cylinder and creating work. Diesel had created the most efficient internal combustion engine yet produced, an engine which converted fuel directly into energy.

Diesel's wife persuaded him to name the new engine after himself, and he began advertising to prospective buyers while improving its design. The engine proved popular, especially among German military leaders with a growing fleet of submarines. On September 29, 1913, Diesel boarded a ferry to cross the English Channel and promote his engine in Britain. When the ferry reached England the next morning, however, Diesel was not on board. A few days later a Dutch fishing vessel picked a body

out of the channel, stripped it of valuables, and threw it back. A pair of glasses from the body eventually reached Diesel's son, who identified them as his father's. Authorities never confirmed Diesel's death, however, causing much speculation about his disappearance.

Whatever his fate, Diesel never saw his engine revolutionize the shipping and railroad industries. In World War I several nations used lightweight diesel engines in submarines and surface ships. After the war, shippers quickly adopted the engine for merchant fleets.

The use of diesels on land proceeded more slowly. In the 1920s some American urban and short line railways began using gas engines in passenger rail cars. The engines powered electric generators which ran traction motors connected to the axles of the cars. The engines only developed about 400 horsepower, however, and the cars could not pull trains.

David Driscoll/SRHA collection

This view, looking north from the footbridge joining Spencer and East Spencer, shows more than southbound train No. 29 on Sept. 28, 1947. In the distance are the Spencer depot and yard switcher No. 1742.

North Carolina Division of Archives and History

Diesels approach the roundhouse from the south (right) in the late 1940s. Note (far right) steam locomotives at the 1912 turntable and smoke (top left) coming from smoke jacks in roundhouse roof.

In 1932 Charles W. Kettering, an engineer with General Motors' Electro-Motive Division (EMD), developed a lightweight diesel engine which generated over 1,000 horsepower. Electro-Motive combined the engine, generators, and traction motors in an aerodynamic body to create the first diesel-electric locomotive. In 1934 the Chicago, Burlington and Quincy Railroad ordered one for its Zephyr passenger train. Soon the Union Pacific and other western railroads ordered units for their passenger trains. Because of the relative scarcity of coal in much of the West, railroads there were willing to take a chance on the "diesels," as the new locomotives were called, even though their long-term capacity for service and low maintenance was unproven.

Eastern railroads approached diesels tentatively. In 1939 Southern

president Ernest Norris ordered six 750-horsepower diesels for short-line passenger trains in the Deep South. On September 24 the Goldenrod, Southern's first diesel passenger train, began service between Columbus, Mississippi, and Mobile, Alabama. Company officials were so pleased that they ordered 12 larger diesels for long-distance passenger trains.

Despite success with passenger trains, railroads remained skeptical that diesels could pull more freight than steam engines. This was significant since passenger traffic was declining due to competition from planes and autos while freight traffic held steady. The Electro-Motive Division set out to change this in 1939 with its FT demonstrator No. 103, the first road-freight diesel locomotive. Its four units together produced 5,400 horsepower, more than

any contemporary steam engine. EMD sent its new locomotive on an 83,000-mile, year-long demonstration run on 20 different railroads in 30 states. The FT 103 pulled heavier loads than a steam engine at half the fuel cost. Ironically, an automobile maker (General Motors) had built America's first successful diesel locomotive.

Southern officials were so impressed by the FT demonstrator No. 103's performance that when the tests were over they bought it outright and put it into service as Southern 6100 on May 26, 1941. Several other freight diesels soon joined Southern's roster.

The diesels were expensive, but Southern officials decided they would be more productive in the long run than new steam engines. The diesels used less fuel, pulled greater loads, and

Posing in front of diesel switcher No. 2010 are flagman W. E. Harris Jr., brakeman Henry Greenway, conductor Ted Sharp, road foreman J. Sink, fireman Poteat, and engineer "Bull" Faschnecht.

into Spencer Shops the workers had heard a great deal about it—enough to dread its arrival. "The first time I ever saw one of 'em pull in here I knew it was going to be the end of the steam locomotive," recalls Charlie Peacock, a retired brakeman. "And I knew it was going to be the end of a lot of jobs." He adds that Jake Weant, a veteran boilermaker, observed that all the diesels should be run into the Yadkin River. "He knew the boilermaker's job was going to be short-lived. And of course it was." The shopmen were well aware that interchangeable diesel parts severely reduced the need for custom parts and craftsmanship. Retired laborer Brad Stillman recalls an "old man Peeler" with whom he worked, noting that, while the diesels promised cleaner work, "there were going to be a lot of people out of jobs."

needed less maintenance. They could even be repaired more cheaply because their parts, nearly all interchangeable, could be bought in large quantities from manufacturers. Southern executives opted for total "dieselization" and would achieve this goal in June 1953, the first major railroad to do so.

By the time the first diesel rolled

It seemed for several years after Southern's first diesel purchase that shopmen need not have worried.

This Sept. 15, 1946, view shows a back shop full of steam engines and a few diesels.

Ties *magazine*

R. M. Barnett (left) and Frank Sides inspect a diesel engine filter in a room created during conversion of the roundhouse for diesel repairs.

World War II severely curtailed the railway's acquisition of diesels, and the company had to work its still formidable steam fleet to the point of exhaustion. The number of employees at Spencer reached an all-time high during the war just to keep the locomotives on the road. After the war ended, the railroad began extensive renovation at the shops to service diesels. All the attention convinced some workers that the shops and most of the jobs would survive the diesel transition.

Between 1948 and 1950 Southern renovated stalls 17 through 37 (the right side) of the roundhouse, adding features to allow thorough inspection and repair of diesels. Inspection and repair continued in stalls 29 through 37 while 17 through 28 became "rooms" for a variety of purposes. To form the rooms workers took up the tracks, filled in the pits, poured a concrete floor, and made walls from old boxcar roofing. A large room made from stalls 17 to 21 contained equipment for repairing diesel batteries. In an adjoining room coils in the steam generators of diesel passenger locomotives were rewound. Passenger cars during the steam era

David Driscoll/SRHA collection

By late May 1949 Spencer was well on its way to becoming dieselized. Here a four-unit set of freight engines idles beneath a new sand facility for diesels as steam locomotives simmer nearby.

Ties *magazine*

As diesels came on line, Southern converted the flue shop to an electrical shop with a neat arrangement of storage cabinets and work benches.

were heated with steam from locomotive boilers. When diesels began to pull passenger trains, steam generators were installed in the new locomotives to provide steam to heat the cars. Later passenger cars had electric heat, and steam generators were not needed. Another wall between stalls 28 and 29 created a room where workers cleaned oil filters and other heavily soiled parts.

Rooms previously built onto the back of the roundhouse changed purpose around the time of the diesel conversion. The machine shop, built in 1924, became a locker and rest room for white employees. The original locker room had been behind the left side of the roundhouse between it and the blacksmith shop.

A room built in 1942 between the roundhouse machine shop and the ticket office originally served as a pipe shop where workers cleaned and repaired air, water, sand, and lubricant lines on steam locomotives. During or not long after the diesel conversion, the room became a segregated locker room for black workers. Doors on the adjacent locker rooms were labeled "white" and "colored." According to

Spencer retirees, locker facilities were integrated in the 1960s, though both rooms served no other function while the shops operated.

Diesels were generally longer than their steam counterparts and frequently presented a space dilemma frequently when converting aging steam facilities to diesel capability. Southern solved the problem at the

Spencer roundhouse by moving the rear wall back 26 feet in stalls 29 through 37. The floor was cemented and longer rails installed, but the most drastic change showed how different diesel repair would be. Wooden platforms were built in each stall which ran almost the entire length of a diesel locomotive. The platforms were built level to the doors on the sides of the locomotives to allow easy access to the engines inside. Employees could step directly inside a locomotive and remove heavy parts or machines without having to lift or lower them to a work area.

In 1948 company engineers built a drop pit under stalls 29-32 to drop diesel wheel sets. A fully motorized drop table lowered wheel sets from locomotives and carried them to a release track in stall 29.

Extending the back wall of the roundhouse allowed for creation of a small machine shop and an office for the roundhouse foreman. The new machine shop's small size revealed the reduced need for machining in diesel repair. More storage and office space was created from the old boiler wash house which became part of the

David Driscoll/SRHA collection

It's Sept. 15, 1946, and both steam and diesel share the back shop. Alco diesel switcher No. 6001 is without a motor or trucks in this view.

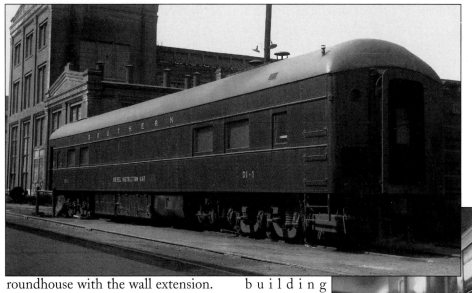

Both: David Driscoll/SRHA collection

Left: By October 1945 Southern was teaching employees all about diesels with a special car, diesel instruction car No. DI-1, based at Spencer. Here it sits by a shop building whose marquee-like sign reads: Southern Ry. Spencer Shop.

Below: Inside diesel instruction car No. DI-1, in use by late 1945, was a model of diesel No. 4100 (with wheels which turned relative to trainees' use of a test throttle) and a control stand mockup.

roundhouse with the wall extension.

While the roundhouse remained a locomotive repair and service center, the flue shop changed completely. Diesels contained a maze of electrical wiring and components, and the shops needed more room for electrical work. The flue shop, by 1953 as obsolete as steam engine flues, was an ideal site. Southern installed new equipment for testing and repairing diesel electrical systems, and the building became known as the "electric shop." Electricians were the only Spencer workers whose job security was actually strengthened by the conversion to diesels, and Southern had to hire many new apprentice electricians.

With the arrival of the diesel the mighty back shop, symbol of steam era repair, could have been abandoned or faced the wrath of the wrecking ball. In 1947 Southern planned a new diesel shop for Spencer. The new complex, to contain a storehouse, machine shop, wheel drop pit, and covered work area, was to be built north of the master mechanic's office. Then Southern officials decided instead to convert the existing back shop to repair of diesels.

The conversion took place not long after the roundhouse renovation. The basic structure of the back shop stayed unchanged, but work there underwent a small revolution. The erecting shop on the west side of the building remained the area where locomotives undergoing overhaul were stripped of their parts. The huge overhead cranes lifted diesels as easily as steam locomotives and were used frequently. The storage pits for steam parts were filled in, as most parts removed from diesels were taken to the electric shop or machine shop and reinstalled immediately upon their return. Southern turned the machine shop in the east side of the back shop into a assembly-disassembly line for giant diesel engines plucked from the bodies of the locomotives. New machines for testing engine components joined the already crowded shop floor.

The flurry of renovation spread to other areas of the shops. By the mid-1950s wooden cars had all but disappeared, and with them went the need for a woodworking shop. But the building received a new lease on life when workers installed machines for refurbishing axles and wheels from diesels. The machines and work space were sorely needed because most diesels contained many more axles and wheels than steam locomotives.

The only structure made completely obsolete by the diesels was the imposing 110-foot-high coal chute built in 1913. Millions of tons of coal had passed through the chute, but by 1953, when Southern's last steam engine was retired, it was a ghost of a bygone age. On June 8 a demolition team dynamited the base of the chute. The old structure fell reluctantly to the ground, and it and the coal storage area were dismantled and removed.

Refueling diesels required no elaborate towers. In 1949 a diesel fueling and sanding station was built at the inspection tracks. It operated on the same principles as gas pumps at an auto service station and was built at the inspection tracks so that a locomotive could be inspected and prepared for its next run simultaneously. Underground piping connected new one-million-gallon fuel tanks to hoses at the station with which laborers refueled the diesels. The workers used other hoses to fill locomotive sandboxes with sand from small, elevated sanding towers built beside the tracks. The dried sand arrived at the site in large paper bags. Laborers emptied the bags into underground storage tanks, and compressed air forced the sand through vertical pipes to the towers. The sand house, where sand formerly had been dried and stored, fell into disuse. It stands at the site today, barely touched by human hands since its abandonment more than 40 years ago.

The paint shop changed location during the diesel conversion, though for an unexpected reason. Early one morning in 1950 the building caught fire and burned over five hours despite the efforts of the shops' fire crews. To replace it, management converted the increasingly obsolete tender repair shed. After minor modifications (such as roof vents to allow paint fumes to escape) the painters moved into the building while tender repair moved to a small shed near the roundhouse. The new paint shop contained sanders and paint sprayers to strip and reapply paint to the tremendous surface area of the diesels.

The oil house, blacksmith, and boiler shops and master mechanic's office were not affected by the initial diesel conversion except for addition of new machines used in diesel repairs. The car repair shed was not threatened, but newer freight cars, like diesels, could travel greater distances between repairs, creating an ominous decline in work to be done.

With the conversion of buildings and facilities complete, Southern faced an even greater challenge, converting the minds of the Spencer workers. Rarely has the maintenance force of an industry faced a more drastic change than that of the railroad shops in the 1940s and 1950s. While the frames and bodies of diesels were repaired with welding and sheet metal work as on steam engines, inside components were another matter entirely.

The diesel engines were little different from those of trucks and automobiles, and their repair required skills of a mechanic more than a metalsmith. Most other components—traction motors, electric and steam generators, batteries, and alternators—were completely new to the shopmen.

Southern and other railroads launched a massive retraining effort to teach shopmen and train crews how to run and repair the new motive power. Company officials were particularly eager to give young supervisors intense training in diesel operation. They hoped to create a new generation of middle and upper management to lead the company into the future. Young men, managers believed, were more likely to embrace the new technology than old men who had worked with steam throughout their careers.

The men picked for the program went to diesel factories in Illinois and New York and immersed themselves in intense training provided by the manufacturers. Upon returning, they shared their new knowledge with shopmen and train crews on the job or in classrooms formerly used to train apprentices. Foremen in each department also went to manufacturers' training sessions. To supplement company training, many shopmen took courses from the International Correspondence School. Managers, foremen, and craftsmen all devoured instruction books and poured over every inch of the diesels, learning about parts and procedures. New knowledge meant job security.

Locomotive engineers likewise needed intense training to master the diesels. In 1945 Southern built its first diesel instruction (DI) cars. They contained working exhibits of diesel components such as electrical cabinets, fuel pumps and tanks, traction motors, and a cutaway model of a 350-horsepower diesel engine. The DI cars, one for the eastern and one

Ties *magazine*

Electricians such as A. E. Everhart, shown in 1953, removed parts from diesel locomotives and took them to the electrical shop for repair or rebuilding.

for the western and central lines, traveled to shops and terminals across the system. J. F. Sheneman, a Salisbury native and diesel instructor, accompanied the cars and held classes at each stop with slides, silent movies, and the working models. For engineers, one section of the DI cars simulated an engineer's chair and controls in diesel cabs. The throttle, transition, and reverse levers operated wheels on a scale model of a freight locomotive so students could see simulated wheel action of an actual unit. Shopmen studied full-size braking and electrical equipment, much of it operational.

Each of Sheneman's classes averaged about ten students, and by 1949 he had conducted over a thousand classes in the eastern lines car alone. In most cases, neither shopmen nor train crews were required to attend classes. Yet those who did so wisely saw it as the quickest way to learn more about their jobs and increase their job security. Diesel technology advanced so rapidly that equipment in the DI cars was soon obsolete. Southern converted some old Pullman cars into DI cars with more current equipment and had them in use by 1953.

While conversion of the shops

David Driscoll/SRHA collection

One job at the back shop was rebuilding wrecks. On Sept. 19, 1949, train No. 15 derailed at Newton, N.C., with locomotives No. 4134 and 4352 and 10 cars, killing three and injuring 29. This view shows a wreck train arriving to pick up the wreckage. The diesels are at the lower left of the photo.

and retraining of shopmen continued, the number of steam locomotives passing through the site dwindled steadily. Most of those based at Spencer were lined up end-to-end and slowly pushed north in great caravans to be cut up at the scrapyards of Chicago and Pittsburgh. "When they lined them engines up... , some of these old fellas, tears came in their

eyes," recalls Jim Misemore, a retired roundhouse foreman.

On June 17, 1953, Southern's last regularly operating steam locomotive, No. 6330, pulled solemnly into the Chattanooga yard. Its fires were killed and its boiler went cold for the final time; Southern had become the first major railroad in the nation to fully dieselize.

No Southern employee of any rank could easily comprehend the dramatic changes which the diesels had brought in the 14 short years since the arrival of the first two diminutive passenger units. By 1953 880 diesels, costing over $123 million, were doing the work of more than twice that number of steam engines. The diesels' phenomenal durability, in addition to their great strength, allowed this feat. Each passenger diesel averaged 14,000 service miles per month, 300 percent more than the old steam locomotives. Freight diesels doubled the monthly mileage of their steam counterparts, while yard diesels averaged 7,000 hours a year, a 136 percent increase over steam switchers. While steam locomotives had received maintenance checks every 150 to 200 miles, some diesels logged over 4,000 miles between checks.

The diesels' tremendous durability ended the policy of operating locomotives only over one or two districts within a division. Spencer's steam locomotives had rarely traveled more than 200 miles—to Greenville, Monroe, or Asheville, for example—before receiving light maintenance and turning around for a return trip. By 1953 freight diesels operated over

David Driscoll/SRHA collection

Less than a month after the wreck of No. 15, Spencer workers were well underway with rebuilding No. 4134. The engine is shown here, stripped to its framework, in the back shop on Oct. 16, 1949.

an entire region. Diesels based at Spencer might go all the way to Washington or Atlanta and back before a maintenance check. Some passenger locomotives ran over portions of two or even all three of Southern's operating regions as part of their regular routes.

Perhaps the greatest changes of the diesel era were reserved for Southern's shop system. At the peak of steam in the 1930s and early 1940s Southern had six heavy repair shops (including Spencer), eight light repair shops, and 19 roundhouses for running repairs. Spencer, heavy repair center for the eastern lines, was supplemented by smaller shops at Columbia and Alexandria. When diesels arrived, they required a completely different type of repair and much less of it. With relatively few diesels on the job, traveling previously unthinkable distances between repairs, the need to reduce shop forces became acute. Due to conversion of the back shop and other buildings, Spencer remained a heavy repair center. The only other shops for heavy repairs and overhaul by 1953 were the Pegram Shops in Atlanta. The Knoxville, Chattanooga, and Birmingham shops, heavy repair facilities in the steam era, were relegated to inspections and periodic maintenance. Thirteen other sites across the system could perform inspections and light maintenance if necessary. One of these was a small rectangular complex built in Alexandria in 1945 specifically for diesels. It was a prototype of the diesel shop designed for Spencer in 1947 but never built. A new shop designed for diesel repair did open at Chattanooga, an ominous sign for Spencer workers, though few recognized it at the time.

As one of two remaining heavy repair shops on the Southern system, it appeared Spencer Shops had a secure future. The diesels had brought great changes, but most shopmen understood the need for change. The greater strength and efficiency of diesels allowed major railroads like Southern to keep their heads above water in the furious battle against

In 1953 a local high school visited Spencer for the Rowan County bicentennial. The back shop had been converted for diesel repair. Diesel engines and bodies filled the giant building where steam had once been supreme.

trucks and pipelines for the nation's freight traffic. Spencer shopmen were famous throughout the Southern system for their ingenuity and occasional miracles with wrecked and problem locomotives. They could adapt to a revolution in shop work, if anyone could. The shopmen were glad to have survived the first wave of the diesel revolution, but the more perceptive among them warned that the most far-reaching changes lay in the future.

Locomotive Repair in the Diesel Era— an Overview

The durable diesels were not taken to the roundhouse or back shop after each run. Most, however, were taken to the inspection pits via the roundhouse lead just like steam locomotives. If inspectors found no problems and the locomotive was not scheduled for periodic maintenance, it was simply fueled and sanded and taken by a hostler to the ready tracks for another run.

If the inspectors or crew found a problem or further inspection was required, the locomotive was put into one of the eight stalls of the round-

house converted for diesel repair. Passenger locomotives had a quick bath at the wash track before entering the building.

Inspection and repair on diesels differed radically from that on steam engines. Craftsmen joked that on a steam locomotive it took six minutes to find a problem and six hours to fix it, while on a diesel it took six hours to find a problem and six minutes to fix it. Craftsmen examined noises, discharges, and other signs to determine which component of a complex diesel was defective. Electricians sometimes pored over miles of wiring for many minutes to locate a simple short or faulty connection. Once found, a problem was often within a part which could simply be replaced with a new one kept on hand at the site. When it was more cost effective to fix the part, equipment in the small machine shop enabled shopmen to manipulate metal or re-bore cylinders just as they had with steam locomotives.

On inspections, craftsmen examined the seemingly endless parts inside the locomotive's body. They followed air, water, fuel, and oil lines searching for problems and checked filters which purified the same substances. Dirty oil and fuel filters were removed for cleaning, as were batter-

The daily grind at Spencer changed forever when diesels replaced steam locomotives such as these shown lined up in March 1952 for the trip to an Illinois scrapyard.

ies and steam generators. Shopmen checked pistons, valves, cylinders, manifolds, injectors, radiators, and pumps on diesel engines and replaced them if necessary. Electric generators were taken apart and the copper coils rewound. Wheels could be removed at the drop pit and taken to the wheel shop. Checks of air brake and lighting systems, fans, doors and windows, and the engineer's controls rounded out inspections in the roundhouse. As in the steam era, the transportation department dictated which locomotives received priority repair and inspection. This was simpler, however, since only eight stalls held locomo-

tives at any time and there were far fewer diesels.

Following inspection or repair, diesels could be started and moved quickly to the ready tracks, freight yard, or depots without the lengthy firing-up period required for steam locomotives.

Overhauls

By the time the back shop had been converted for diesel overhauls, Southern had learned through trial and error that diesels needed complete overhauls every million miles. While this number may seem unusually large, the fact that only the Spencer

and Pegram Shops (in Atlanta) were equipped for full overhauls kept enough locomotives coming through to keep Spencer shopmen busy.

Diesels entered the erecting shop portion of the back shop on the communication track as their steam-powered cousins had done before them. Overhead cranes removed the engines from the locomotive bodies and then removed the bodies from the wheels. The engines were carried to the machine shop side of the building and placed on flanged-wheel dollies which rolled on the track which ran down the middle of the shop.

Beginning at the building's north end, the engines rolled from station to station while shopmen systematically dismantled them. Some of the stations were built so men could work on three levels, simultaneously removing parts from the top, bottom, and sides of the engines. Some of the machines and equipment at the stations, in particular the devices which inverted the engines for removal of crankshafts, were built at Spencer.

Parts removed from engines were taken to testing and reconditioning areas. Pistons, for example, were taken apart and each piece cleaned and inspected. Fuel injectors, air compressors, water pumps, and even crankshafts underwent testing on special machines installed during the diesel conversion. Some bent or worn parts and housings were reclaimed by weld-

North Carolina Division of Archives and History
Southern FT diesel No. 4111 sits on blocks in the back shop.

David Driscoll/SRHA collection

Southern discovered that a few diesels could do the work of many steam locomotives. By 1953 there would be 880 diesels and no steam locomotives in regular service.

ing or machining, but most were simply replaced with new ones kept in stock much like the parts at an automobile garage. Parts on most diesels were made to standard sizes and were almost certain to fit.

For reassembly, the station-to-station order was reversed with most work done across the aisle from the dismantling stations. By the time an engine was reassembled it was where it had begun the dismantling process, ready for return to its respective locomotive.

While the engine was undergoing inspection and repair, the locomotive body received a thorough check. Shopmen attacked dents and scratches with welders, putty, and sanders. Air compressors, fuel injectors, brakes, radiators, and generators received attention in the back shop at designated areas which stocked testing and repair equipment. Wheels were removed to the wheel shop (the old woodworking shop) where machines gave them new surfaces.

Shopmen removed electrical equipment and motors from locomotives for repair at the electric shop in the former flue shop building. Electricians there tested cables and motors on equipment designed and built at the site. Spencer electricians could overhaul any electrical component except traction motors and main generators. These were sent to Atlanta's Pegram Shops, the only Southern facility equipped to overhaul them.

When all parts had been inspected, tested, repaired or replaced, and returned, the locomotive was re-

assembled in the erecting shop. It was then removed from the back shop and tested before being returned to service. Inspectors took each locomotive for a brief trial run, and any problems they noted were corrected by the person in charge of the original overhaul of the parts involved. Most overhauled locomotives needed repainting in the new and spacious paint shop (in the old tank shop building). Once all work was approved and new paint and lettering had been applied, the locomotive was fueled and sanded at the inspection pits and taken to the ready tracks to await assignment.

By the mid-1950s Spencer's buildings had been equipped to prosper in railroading's new era, and the shopmen had abandoned life-long techniques for new ones. Like medical doctors suddenly forced to be veterinarians, the shopmen had struggled to learn how to mend a totally different animal. Around 1500 men still worked at the shops, half the number there during World War II but about the same as through much of the steam era.

In spite of the success of the diesel conversion, several problems proved insurmountable. The craft jurisdiction system, which in the steam era had relegated all tasks and all parts to the auspices of particular crafts, had become a glaring anachronism. The national craft unions, which had helped create the jurisdiction system, were slow to adopt new rules for diesels. The craftsmen tried valiantly to adjust on their own. For example, pipefitters worked with any piping found in the diesels, and boilermakers

handled welding duties. This arrangement proved difficult to maintain, though, because diesel repairs did not easily fit the old jurisdiction system.

The machinists enjoyed an advantage in the conversion since their steam-era skills transferred more easily to diesel repair. Some other craftsmen complained that machinists were claiming an inordinate number of tasks. The resentment was rooted in the belief that jobs and careers were at stake. The craftsmen guessed (correctly) that if mass layoffs were to occur seniority might take a back seat to usefulness. The unions could fight it, but railroads would argue that they could only survive by releasing workers made obsolete by the diesels. As a result, pipefitters, boilermakers, tinsmiths, and blacksmiths desperately struggled to prove their continued worth.

As a new nationwide jurisdiction system was not forthcoming from unions or companies, the animosity between crafts festered and grew. A few retired workers believe the squabbling helped lead to the demise of Spencer Shops. The actual role problems of craft jurisdiction played in the ultimate closing of the shops is difficult to determine as it occurred over several long and painful years and involved complex, intertwined events.

Jim Wrinn

Diesels such as this early 1950s FP7 were the main reason for Spencer's demise. Ironically the locomotive later would join the museum collection at a new Spencer.

The Demise of Spencer Shops

11

Fate caught up with Spencer workers in the mid-1950s, not long after the shops became one of Southern's two remaining heavy repair complexes. Railroad work had always been seasonal, and men lower in seniority were accustomed to layoffs of days or weeks at a time if business ebbed. In most cases, though, men laid off since the arrival of the diesels had not been called back. Increasingly men were called into a foreman's office only to emerge with a pink slip and the advice, "Don't call us, we'll call you." As they had feared, the more anachronistic crafts, such as boiler-makers and black-smiths, felt the layoffs more harshly.

Beginning in late 1957 layoffs grew at an alarming rate. Some laid-off workers apprenticed as electri-cians, the only craft considered "safe." Others became labor-ers or helpers in the car repair shed which briefly was a flurry of activity. Southern decided to convert a fleet of aging boxcars into open pulpwood cars and chose the Spencer car shed for the job. Hundreds of men busily dismantled boxcars, rebuilt them, and fitted them with new brakes and wheels, but the scene was deceiving. There were actually fewer regular repairs made at the sheds because newer cars needed them less frequent-ly, and Southern was shifting many repairs to its primary car facility in Spartanburg, South Carolina. When the boxcar conversion ended, there would be excess workers. The awful consequences of the situation stewed in the mind of each worker as he labored in the sheds.

Out-of-work shopmen often found it difficult to obtain jobs in other area industries. Local compa-nies knew the men would return to higher paying railroad jobs if given the opportunity and considered it a liability to hire and train them. Many men simply waited to be called back, but others, realizing the wait would be long, responded to Southern's offer of positions (often unskilled) in other

North Carolina Division of Archives and History

This diesel powered streamliner at Spencer was emblematic of the switch from steam to internal combustion power.

areas. Every morning several men from Spencer and East Spencer hopped a train for the hour-long ride to the Charlotte or Greensboro termi-nals where they would work a full day then ride back in the evening. They were no longer shopmen, but they were still railroaders. That, at least, was something.

Shopmen were not the only rail-road workers whose ranks were thinned by the efficiency of diesel operations. The fireman's job was an obvious anachronism but firemen's unions across the country fought stubbornly to protect their jobs. Their struggle with Southern began in the mid-1950s not long after William "Bill" Brosnan became the company's vice-president of operations. Brosnan was a career railroad man with a rep-utation as a hard-nosed efficiency expert and was completely dedicated to the company's success. He was the type of manager Southern desperately needed to survive increasingly strin-gent government regulation and harsh competition from the burgeoning trucking industry. Brosnan deter-mined to take full advantage of the efficiency of diesels, and this meant elimi-nating every obsolete employee. Brosnan declined to lay off working firemen but refused to hire new ones in anticipation that retirement and attrition would eventu-ally leave no firemen. For the national fire-men's union this was a dangerous precedent. If all the large railroads rid themselves of firemen, the craft itself would disappear. Faced with imminent demise, the union turned to the courts. After a bitter and protracted legal battle, a federal judge ordered Brosnan to hire new firemen. Undaunted, he turned the tables on the union. The new firemen he hired were elderly, mostly black, and as like-ly to be women as men. Brosnan admitted later that he was trying to prove that "anyone, regardless of age, race, sex, education, or state of health, could do the job—sitting in a com-fortable seat." For several months many confounded engineers in diesel cabs looked over to the fireman's chair

David Driscoll/SRHA collection

The dismal process of dismantling steam engines saw headlights and number plates tossed into piles. Today this would be a collectors dream! Here headlights for Nos. 4830, 1855, 5028, 1083, 1631, and 567 await their fate.

North Carolina Division of Archives and History

The mighty back shop had been abandoned for years in 1977 when Southern donated it the state for a museum, and nature was reclaiming the site.

only to see politely smiling, elderly black women. The engineers smiled back but gritted their teeth. Brosnan was a force to be reckoned with.

The firemen's union rushed back to the courts, but Brosnan argued, and the court agreed, that he had the right to choose whom he would hire as firemen and define their duties. He reasoned that if he had to waste money hiring unnecessary employees it should go to people who really needed it. The union did not appreciate Brosnan's "generosity" but was largely helpless to change it. In 1972 the union and Southern finally agreed that new firemen would be hired but only as a source of future engineers.

The battle with the firemen was only a small part of Brosnan's efforts to cut costs and increase efficiency. His sharp eye spared no part of the line's vast operating systems, but he paid particular attention to shops, the department most affected by dieselization. Brosnan was a pragmatist and learned from successes of the enemy, in this case the automobile industry. He analyzed productivity on the assembly lines of General Motors and lured away several young engineers to create the same efficiency in Southern's shops. One such engineer, Richard Hamilton, found work cut out for him. "In each shop they thought they had to be able to do everything," he recalled. "We had forced centralization and then we got some volume. I closed a lot of shops and cut hell out of the employees. I knew what needed to be done." Hamilton was joined by a former machinist and Brosnan protege, Dick Franklin. It was they who closed several smaller shops and introduced spot inspection and repair methods adopted at Spencer and other remaining shops during the 1950s. These meth-

ods, modeled after auto assembly lines, greatly increased productivity.

Yet Hamilton and Franklin were not finished. They studied the heavy repair facilities at Spencer and Atlanta to determine if more efficiency could be squeezed out of the overhaul process. Perhaps only they know the true reasons behind their next decision, to enlarge shops at Atlanta and Chattanooga but close down heavy repair and overhaul at Spencer. New buildings and equipment would

BULLETIN   BULLETIN

                          Spencer, N.C., November 2, 1956.

To All Employees:

    Referring to Mr. C. D. Schwine's and Mr. H. C. Swanson's
bulletin of November 1st, 1956, about reduction in forces in the
Locomotive Department at Spencer, N.C., effective 7:15 A.M.,
November 6th, 1956:

    The following men will be affected:

Machinist Helpers

J. A. Waddell
E. D. Isenhour
R. C. Leslie

Boilermaker Helper

H. D. Simerson

Laborers

John Smith
S. J. Harrison

                                    O. H. Smart
                                    Assistant Master Mechanic
Post -

Machine Shop:
Wheel Shop:
Diesel Shop:
Roundhouse:
Car Shop:
Boiler Shop:

North Carolina Division of Archives and History
Layoff notices appeared continually during the 1950s. The number of men affected varied from a few to several hundred.

increase productivity of diesel overhauls, but it would be at Chattanooga, not Spencer.

In later years nearly every former shop worker and resident of Spencer offered an explanation why the shops were shut down. Many believed Spencer natives who had worked up to high management positions had kept the shops open. Brosnan and other officials "had it in for" Spencer Shops, they claimed, and when the Spencer natives retired in the late 1950s, this left Brosnan free to do as he pleased. When pressed for a reason why officials might have held animos-

ity toward Spencer, a few suggested that the heated squabbles between crafts about jurisdiction over diesel repairs had fostered management's wrath. Firemen, boilermakers, and other workers who "featherbedded," or insisted on keeping obsolete jobs, were also cited as causes.

Other Spencer residents said such problems occurred all over the system, and there was no reason to single out Spencer as a target. They claimed the company would not have made an inefficient move simply due to an emotional vendetta. Pure economics caused the move, they said. Could a complex built during the steam era become a truly productive diesel center adaptable to future changes? The most accurate explanation for Spencer's demise seems to be a combination of all of the above. The drive for greater economy already had resulted in vast changes in day-to-day operations and closing of many Southern facilities. Further closings seemed inevitable. Yet it is clear that Spencer had been the focus of attention by Southern's highest officials for some time. A company-blessed history of the railway states that, when Franklin told him of the decision to close Spencer, Brosnan replied, "I've been trying to get out of that place for years." Through 1958 and 1959 the layoffs and transfers continued at Spencer, but actually shutting the shops down presented Franklin and Hamilton with a problem. Closing such a large and venerated facility would raise the ire not only of the Spencer shopmen but of employees throughout the system. The solution came from an unexpected source.

As early as 1955 the North Carolina Department of Water Resources had asked Southern for a plan to prevent oil and other shops wastes from seeping into the Yadkin River. Franklin ultimately recognized in the request a golden opportunity.

Nervous shopmen and townspeople, anxiously waiting to see what steps the railroad would take next, got their answer on July 27, 1960, when Robert Barnett, shop superintendent, posted a notice that 179 men would be laid off the following Saturday. The layoff would take every man from the back shop as well as the blacksmith, boiler, and paint shops, leaving only the roundhouse and car sheds functioning. Around 25 men would remain at the roundhouse for light maintenance on switch engines and any locomotives which developed trouble passing through the area. "This is not a temporary layoff," a company official told reporters. "The transfer of engine overhaul and heavy maintenance work to Atlanta and Chattanooga started more than a year ago, and this is the final close-down of the back shop." A second announcement the next day cut the work force at the car sheds from 66 to 50, leaving around 75 workers at the site. Only seven years earlier there had been more than 1500.

The Spencer Shops had effectively shut down. The car sheds and roundhouse were open, at greatly reduced capacity, only because the freight yard remained in operation, and inspection and repair facilities were required anywhere cars and locomotives were being switched. Brosnan, after consultation with Hamilton and Richards, answered outraged citizens and civic leaders of Spencer who demanded to know the reasons for the shutdown. The state Department of Water Resources, he said, had made "unreasonable" demands for waste treatment facilities at the site. The railroad had offered to build a $90,000 facility to remove oily wastes, Brosnan said, but state engineers had demanded a much more comprehensive facility costing at least

Marvin Rogers

It's the morning after the Southern Crescent derailed at Spencer in 1977. The locomotives are still askew on the ground.

$120,000. E. C. Hubbard of the Department of Water Resources had insisted that the railroad submit plans for action by August 15, 1960, a nonnegotiable date. Faced with the choice of building an "unreasonable" facility or closing the site, Brosnan indicated, the company had chosen the latter with much regret. He concluded by reminding town officials that many laid-off men were being offered positions elsewhere in the system and promised that the company would help attract other industries to lease

the shop buildings and again provide the town with an industrial base.

Brosnan's letter elicited an immediate reply from none other that Hubbard, who made sure that his letter to Brosnan found its way into the *Salisbury Post* on August 2. Hubbard reminded Brosnan that the railroad had set all deadlines and submitted all cost estimates for the treatment facilities. The company had offered a $90,000 facility to remove some wastes but refused to build a $120,000 complex to remove all of them.

Marvin Rogers

We're at the north end of Spencer Yard the day after the Southern Crescent derailed in 1977.

A 1982 view shows the inside of once busy back shop as a scene of silence and decay.

Hubbard saw no logic in this. "Based upon your own figures," he wrote, "it would appear unreasonable to assume that a large and responsible company such as the Southern Railway System would relocate a facility of this size and importance solely to avoid spending an additional $30,000 to provide necessary treatment of all wastes for the protection of public health." He added that his office had been "more than lenient" with Southern regarding the matter. Hubbard told reporters that the company's charges that his office helped prompt the closing were a "smokescreen" for its real motives.

Southern did not respond publicly and seemed to have little else to say about the situation, leaving state officials fuming. Governor Luther Hodges, notified of the shops' closing by officials of Spencer and Rowan County, began calling the railway's main offices to urge the company to change its mind. "You can't do that," he said when he finally reached Dick Franklin. "The hell I can't," Franklin replied and abruptly ended the conversation.

The closed shop buildings stayed silent and empty and the town of Spencer fell into gloom. Jobless railroad men swore against the company, the unions, even the federal government, which they felt imposed restrictive, profit-reducing regulations on the railroads. Mayor T. Roy Burdette stressed that citizens should not dwell on the situation and make a fruitless search for explanations. They should think not about yesterday but tomorrow. "We're going to take this in stride," he told a reporter. "I don't want to build false hopes, but we've a good little town here. The Rowan County Chamber of Commerce is working hard to get a new industry in here, and I don't see why it can't be done. If the people don't get discouraged, we'll keep it going." City manager Quay Smith echoed Burdette. "Certainly it's going to hurt," he said of the closing. "You can't pull a big payroll out of a small city without it being felt. But this town won't dry up. It won't be a ghost town." Burdette also praised the overall relationship of the town with Southern. "The railroad has been good to us," he said, citing the large park in the center of town which Southern had helped finance. "I wouldn't want anyone to be nicer than they have been to us." Some Spencer business owners even felt that the closing was a good thing. The high railroad wages, they suggested, had kept other industries away.

Shop employees offered positions in Atlanta or Chattanooga had mixed feelings. They were glad to keep their high paying positions but reluctant to move their families to new towns. Jim Misemore went to Atlanta but left his family in Rowan County. "I felt terrible," he recalls, "I had just bought a house, and I had a three-year-old daughter." For eleven years Misemore worked in Atlanta and came home on weekends before ultimately returning to Spencer to join the skeleton crew at the roundhouse. John Nesbitt worked in Salisbury at low-paying jobs for a few months but was eventually lured to the Atlanta shops, leaving his family in East Spencer. Willie Biber, a former transfer sheds employee, found a job in Greensboro at another trans-

Marvin Rogers

The yard shanty at the south end of Spencer Yard in the mid-1970s showed tremendous character and clutter. At least no one accused Southern switch crews of being boring. The tiny shack later surrendered to a modern building near the same site.

fer terminal. He saw little of his family in East Spencer but felt the sacrifice was necessary to provide for them.

"When the shops closed, things were terrible around here for a while," recalls Evelyn Krider, whose restaurant across the street from the shops had fed hordes of hungry shopmen.

Southern had pumped an annual payroll of over $8 million into the community. For years the town had the highest per capita income in the state. Now that it was gone, merchants feared they would be the next to pick up and leave.

Through sheer effort, however, the town kept its head above water. In

Marvin Rogers

A night photo shows the brightly illuminated diesel fueling facility at Spencer during the 1960s and 1970s before Southern called it quits at Spencer.

1963 Spencer officials persuaded the railway to sell the park it had maintained across from the shops since the town was founded. The park had once held the baseball field where the shops team played on summer afternoons and the Detroit Tigers and Boston Braves played their famous exhibition game. In the 1920s four community churches landscaped the park. Each church maintained a corner of the park and groomed its trees, flowers, and walkways. The railroad, which had not allowed businesses to locate on the site back in 1896, supplied lights which kept the park lit and safe at night. At its entrance the company placed a large sign bearing its symbol and trademark slogan, "The Southern Serves the South." The town had a beautiful park but also a constant symbol of who owned the land.

The park was a metaphor for Spencer itself. No matter how vibrant and independent the town felt itself to be, it had always been at the mercy of the whims of the Southern Railway. Perhaps persuading the company to sell the park symbolized a final breaking away. The town founded by a railroad company was completely on its own, to survive or fail by its own efforts.

G. B. Nalley, a developer from South Carolina, purchased the park. He constructed a parking lot and a shopping center soon occupied by a grocery store, a department store, and a drugstore relocated from an older building. A new bank opened as well, and the downtown area revived somewhat. Town residents bought stock to build a $65,000 swimming pool, and churches launched building programs for new sanctuaries and education buildings. Spencer did not appear as a community whose lifeblood had been drained away but a vigorous town looking to the future.

Thanks to the loyalty of many railroaders to their hometown, the future would be brighter than anyone had reason to expect. Throughout the 1960s and 1970s retiring railroad men moved back to Spencer and brought with them their lucrative railroad pensions. The pensions helped the town keep the highest average per capita income in the county, a distinction it had held since 1896. Young people still left the town in great numbers, however, seeking the types of jobs the railroad had once promised to many upon graduation from high school. As the young left and retirees returned, the town's population grew steadily older.

The End of an Era

Throughout the 1960s Southern concentrated its remaining repair operations in a few shop buildings and abandoned the rest. Four stalls remained in use at the roundhouse for running repairs on diesel switch engines. In 1964 Southern added a few men to the roundhouse force and increased repairs to freight locomotives operating in the area, but the increase was in significant. Electricians abandoned the old flue shop for a small brick building adjacent to the oil house where they repaired walkie-talkies and small machines used in the roundhouse or freight yard. The oil house became a storehouse, and the old storehouse and master mechanic's office closed down. Activities were concentrated in the oil house because it was near the roundhouse and the fueling-inspection station still in operation.

In 1965 Southern decided to reduce taxable property by removing several unused buildings. The blacksmith, boiler, and wheel shops were dismantled as was most of the car shed. A skeleton crew remained in what was left of the shed, inspecting and making minor repairs to cars switched in the yard. The Marion Machine Company of Marion, North Carolina, reconstructed the boiler shop in Marion and bought much of the heavy equipment not moved to other shops. The railroad held a "yard sale" to relieve itself of other heavy equipment. The transfer sheds shut down in 1970 and were dismantled. Southern seemed to be slowly on its way to ending operations in Spencer entirely.

Yet Spencer residents became very interested when they learned in the mid-1970s that the company planned a large, new freight yard in the area. Surely, they thought, the existing freight yard would simply be enlarged. New jobs seemed headed to the town again. The people's hearts fell when Southern announced it would build a new yard at Linwood, five miles north on the main line, and abandon the Spencer yard. All repair operations at Spencer would then close completely. The once proud back shop and roundhouse would surely meet an ignominious end at the hands of a wrecking ball.

In 1977, however, employees of the North Carolina Department of Cultural Resources introduced the idea of turning the shops into a museum to highlight the history of transportation in the state. Southern was receptive and donated several acres of land and the buildings it was not using to the state. When Linwood Yard was completed in 1979, Southern donated another 57 acres along with all surviving shop buildings, nearly stripped of machinery.

The North Carolina Transportation Museum preserves the heritage of Spencer Shops, shown here in its heyday. Spencer is on the left, and East Spencer is on the right. Note the transfer sheds at bottom right.

Spencer Shops:
The Museum

12

Early in 1996 a construction worker scrawled in the dust on a newly installed roundhouse window: "All good things come to those who wait." The words summed up the almost 20-year struggle to fulfill the promise of Spencer Shops as one of the nation's major transportation museums.

It took a heroic effort, millions of dollars, and hundreds of thousands of hours from museum staff members and volunteers to make the dream come true. But on the shops' centennial, railroad history was to be made once again at Samuel Spencer's namesake. The country's largest standing steam-era roundhouse had been preserved along with 50 pieces of historic rolling stock from across North Carolina and the Southeast. Buildings which once housed the master mechanic's office and flue shop contained museum offices and exhibits. Steam locomotives shuttled around Spencer carrying tourists instead of freight.

Work to restore Spencer Shops began soon after Southern's gift of property in 1979. Department of Cultural Resources employees faced many obstacles. Trees were growing from the old master mechanic's office. Tracks were buried under mud. Weeds, trash, and debris covered the site. Buildings were in sad shape with broken windows, leaky roofs, and rotting timbers after some 20 years of little or no upkeep.

"We didn't even have a place to go to the bathroom," said site manager Don Wooten, one of the original state workers. "We had to go to a store down the street."

They immediately went about the work of putting a new roof on the master mechanic's office and restoring the offices.

Meanwhile the museum's new nonprofit support organization, the North Carolina Transportation History Corporation (NCTHC), was very busy. Site director Allan Paul and NCTHC president J. Fred Corriher Jr. scoured the area for steam locomotives, passenger cars, and other rolling stock for the museum. The task was difficult because, by the late 1970s, few steam engines were left that had not been either preserved or scrapped.

NCTHC's first acquisition, a forlorn steam locomotive in Johnson City, Tennessee, arrived at Spencer in 1978. The group's most significant acquisition came from the hills of southwest Virginia. NCTHC purchased an entire train set—a steam locomotive, tender, baggage car, and several coaches—from the defunct

Southwest Virginia Scenic Railroad. The engine and cars, as well as a diesel switch locomotive that came with the deal, were towed dead to Spencer and put into storage to await the day they would again haul tourists. Other jewels received in the early years were a massive engine built in 1917 for the Russian railways, an ornate business car made for steel magnate Charles Schwab, and a unique country depot from Barber Junction built in 1896.

A consulting firm developed a proposal for a future museum. The roundhouse would contain exhibits on railroading, and restored locomotives and cars would shuttle about the property. The giant back shop would house general transportation exhibits, cars, trucks and airplanes hanging from the ceiling. The million-gallon oil tank at the north end of the property would become a theater in the round. The plan estimated a cost from $12 million to $15 million over five to seven years.

The expectation was set that Spencer would soon blossom into a magnificent museum. Said James Bistline, then head of Southern's law department and a NCTHC board member: "People traveling to Disney World won't get beyond here."

In June 1978 Secretary of Cultural Resources Sara Hodgkins announced the museum would be the department's top priority. More rail

Jim Wrinn

In the early 1980s the museum assembled quite a collection but restored nothing. Here the Barber Junction depot and W. R. Bonsal & Co. locomotive No. 7 rest north of the back shop.

North Carolina Division of Archives and History

N.C Transportation History Corporation president Elmer Lam (left), receives a donation check from Harry Turner of Philip Morris.

equipment arrived including passenger cars, steam locomotives, and two giant green-and-gold diesels from Southern.

The state legislature provided $1.5 million to repair the enormous back shop roof and more money to repair the master mechanic's office. The museum opened its doors in 1980, but it would be three years before visitors had much to see. The venture was gathering steam, but events were already clouding its future. Money for the back shop didn't provide for windows, and strong winds began buckling and causing leaks in the new roof soon after it was finished. Key legislative supporters were defeated in the 1980 election. Allan Paul, the museum's first director, resigned over handling of the project.

Nevertheless positive things began to happen, even as some wondered if the end of the line might finally be near for Spencer Shops.

In 1983 a 6,000-square-foot exhibit called *People, Places and Times* opened in the former storeroom area of the master mechanic's office. The exhibit featured a Native American dugout canoe, early wagons and automobiles, and a homemade airplane. The museum attracted about 4,000 visitors in its first full year of operation.

But the millions of dollars to complete the back shop and roundhouse never came. Legislators introduced bill after bill for major improvements at the museum, only to see them fail time after time. Museum supporters blamed competition from other worthwhile projects, such as the North Carolina Zoo, and concerns that Spencer Shops could cost more than anticipated. The shift in priorities was frustrating to supporters. Money to enclose the back shop after the new roof was installed was not forthcoming. Vandals began to take a toll on engines and cars. They removed the windows from a graceful streamlined Southern diesel, which collected pigeon droppings in the roundhouse.

Then in a heroic turning point for the project, a small group of local people determined that Spencer Shops, the museum, would succeed.

Retired shopmen, many with over 45 years of service, came back in 1985.

Jim Wrinn

J. Fred Corriher Jr., founder of the N.C. Transportation History Corporation, nonprofit support organization for the museum.

Soon after the museum opened, Spencer retirees had begun meeting in a room each week to spin tales of the old days. But these men were different. They'd come to work like they had when they were young, on ancient steam locomotives.

One day at church retired brakeman Charlie Peacock cornered his friend Milton Ruble, a retired foreman. "I told him we had a dead steam locomotive at the museum and asked if he would look at it," Peacock said. "He said, 'sure,' and he and some other fellows and I started to work." Among the volunteers was retired roundhouse foreman Jim Mesimore. He had been the last man in the roundhouse the night it closed as an active repair center in 1979. The locomotive the men focused on was the prize artifact from the Southwest Virginia—a powerful freight engine with two guide wheels and eight drivers. Now it would become the museum's showpiece, a living, breathing steam locomotive. It also would be the ticket to attracting attention. "If we had one steam engine in Spencer, this whole yard would be full of visitors," Spencer Mayor and former boilermaker C. E. "Pappy" Spear told the Salisbury Post. The workers welded and machined the old engine, spending countless hours. "My wife said she used to see me more when I worked for a paycheck than she does now," Ruble said.

The payoff came on July 25, 1986, when, sweating and begrimed, the retired shopmen welcomed 60 invited guests for a short ride in a caboose and restored coach behind the engine they'd labored on so long. The trip, planned to reach 11th Street in Salisbury, was cut short when packing around the air pumps burst into flames. But no one seemed to mind: steam was back at Spencer.

In coming months NCTHC worked hard to make what was a one-shot event a regular occurrence. The

North Carolina Division of Archives and History

The first steam locomotive acquired by the North Carolina Transportation Museum arrives at Spencer Shops in 1978.

nonprofit organization won a grant from Southern's successor, Norfolk Southern Corporation, to rehabilitate tracks at Spencer Shops. A contractor rebuilt a section of track near Barber Junction and reworked the tracks through the shop complex.

A handful of young men interested in railroads stepped forward: con-

struction workers, carpenters, painters, computer programmers, electricians, and even a newspaper writer who saw a need. They tackled the coaches for the train, replacing rotten window frames and painting the cars inside and out.

On a rainy Labor Day weekend in 1987, the museum ran its first excursion train ride. Engineer H. S. "Hot Shot" Williams pulled the throttle, and fireman Lloyd Morris shoveled coal. Conductors Jack Vail and W. C. Hatley punched tickets and talked with passengers. The trip was short—from the master mechanic's office to both ends of the property, a total of three miles. But the rust and weeds once on the tracks were gone, and trains were running on a regular basis for the first time in nearly ten years.

That fall the museum celebrated its tenth anniversary with a restored steam engine and a new sense of vigor. In a few weeks, word about the steam train ride had spread, and more than 6,000 people took the trip.

In shop buildings that had grown quiet, volunteers worked almost daily. "They've changed the whole tenor of the museum," said Wooten. "It hasn't been that long since the trains just sat there. But now they run, thanks to these guys." In one year, 1988, volunteers gave more than 19,000 hours of time, by far the most of any state historic site. "The miracle of Spencer Shops is corporate participation and volunteer enthusiasm," Corriher said. "Both were essential elements needed for the trains to return."

The on-site excursion train began running regularly—on weekends April through December and on spring and summer weekdays. Retirees narrated the trip, telling passengers about the history of Spencer and giving them a chance to meet the people who had actually made history. They gave visitors a ride on the turntable, showing them the giant roundhouse. And then they invited them to walk through the crumbling building, view its antique locomotives and cars, and glimpse volunteers at work in a David-vs.-Goliath effort to restore the worn cars.

Attracted by the steam locomotive, attendance soared. Some 8,600 passengers were carried between September and December. Overall

Volunteers, mainly railroad retirees, pose with the locomotive they restored for the museum's on-site rail ride. The project was a catalyst which caused attendance to soar.

attendance jumped from 3,900 in 1980 to 40,000 in 1984 and 63,000 in 1988. Some 10,000 school children came by the bus load each spring, most for their first train ride.

Still no money came. A proposal for $335,000 in the 1989 session of the legislature died. Supporters became discouraged. The *Salisbury Post* ran a series of articles about the floundering museum, calling it "Spencer Shops…the unfulfilled promise."

The volunteers labored on. In the late 1980s and early 1990s, NCTHC volunteers did cosmetic restorations on important locomotives and rail

cars. Other rolling stock swelled the collection to almost 60 pieces.

The Winston-Salem Chapter of the National Railway Historical Society generously gave a baggage car and coach. In 1991 a chapter grant helped the museum acquire its only Southern Railway steam locomotive, No. 542, displayed in a Forsyth County park since 1954. The Hornets Nest Region of the Antique Automobile Club of America donated money to repaint two giant water tanks on the north end of the property with giant replicas of Southern's famous company emblem.

An important restoration project,

Symbolic of the museum's struggle for money, Seaboard Air Line engine No. 544 rusted at Spencer for more than a dozen years awaiting cosmetic restoration. The project was completed in 1996.

spearheaded by Corriher, was restoration of North Carolina industrialist James B. Duke's private car, the Doris, named after his only daughter. Contractors and volunteers restored the car to the highest working condition so it could roll behind modern Amtrak trains and serve as a good will ambassador for the museum. Money for the work came from grants, individual donors, and fees from train rides.

The museum began a celebration of railroading in 1988 called Rail Days, which became a top fund-raiser. Such events were important because of the high cost of restoring antique rail equipment—$300,000 or so for a private car, and $250,000 for a medium-sized steam locomotive. Attendance at the first event, a one-day affair with steam and diesel train rides, was about 300 people. By 1995 the two-day event, with rides, exhibits, demonstrations, music, and entertainment, drew over 10,000 visitors.

But not everything was fair weather sailing. In September 1989 a mid-Atlantic hurricane named Hugo swept inland creating destruction from Charleston, South Carolina, to Charlotte and on to Bluefield, West Virginia. Damage to the museum was severe. Skylights in the back shop roof were shredded, and the rest of the roof buckled and broke. Ventilators on top of the roundhouse were plucked out and laid on their sides like mushrooms.

The museum grew despite the storm damage, and in 1990 an automobile exhibit opened in the restored flue shop. Governor Jim Martin awarded a $167,000 grant for the project. After fixing the building, craftsmen built dioramas telling the story of the automobile from its inception to the present. Collectors shared cars for the aptly named *Bumper to Bumper* exhibit. Cars from the early years were parked in a barnyard scene, while a

Jim Wrinn

A Southern derrick sets Graham County Railroad Shay engine No. 1925 down in April 1988.

Jim Wrinn

Visitors flooded the museum with each additional offering. *Bumper to Bumper* drew crowds on opening day in July 1991.

Jim Wrinn

A worker with a safety strap dangles high above the floor of the roundhouse repairing concrete in the winter of 1994-95.

Jim Wrinn

A construction worker begins repairs to concrete and windows on the roof of the roundhouse.

two-car garage with a basketball goal represented the 1960s. Again annual visitation jumped, this time to some 80,000.

Still the giant roundhouse and back shop went untouched. But determination was great, and word about Spencer was spreading. The museum received some $200,000 from the legislature to replace the roof, repair broken windows, and repaint the interior of the last five bays of the roundhouse.

Another turning point came in 1992. Over lunch at a Shoney's in Charlotte, a Duke Power Company executive and NCTHC board member named Bob Allen met with other corporation board members to brainstorm ways to get the roundhouse or back shop repaired by 1996, the shops' centennial. Allen, an official with the National Trust for Historic Preservation, suggested seeking money from a new federal highway bill which set aside funds for restoration of historic rail equipment and buildings.

In coming weeks NCTHC board members Dick Messinger and R. O. Everette investigated the matter and asked Governor Martin for help. In July 1992 Deputy Secretary of Transportation Jake Alexander Jr. stood on the steps of the master mechanic's office to give some good news. The museum would receive $4.5 million from the state Department of Transportation. The money would come from the federal Intermodal Surface Transportation Efficiency Act, or ISTEA. NCTHC leased the roundhouse from the state and, working with the Department of Transportation and the Historic Sites Section of the Department of Cultural Resources, worked to restore the building for the centennial.

NCTHC also faced the challenge of raising more money than ever— $1.2 million to qualify for ISTEA's $4-for-$1 matching funds. Led by

Elmer Lam, a retired Dupont executive from Charlotte who became president in November 1992, the organization published a promotional brochure, knocked on doors of individuals and foundations, and approached state officials.

NCTHC sponsored a gala event to demonstrate to area movers and shakers that the museum was back on track. Historic Sites officials created a new exhibit telling about restoration of the roundhouse. The Salisbury Post published coupons so individuals could make donations. Volunteers spread the word about a fund-raising campaign called "Building on the Past, Looking to the Future." The campaign showcased the museum's role as an economic development tool, educational institution, and recreational resource in the middle of the Piedmont, the state's most populated

Jim Wrinn

A spring 1989 photo from the roof of the roundhouse shows four diesels from the museum collection and a lot of work ahead for the roundhouse and back shop (in background).

region. One study placed the museum's economic impact at some $30 million if developed fully.

People responded. Individuals gave $25, $50, and $100 contributions. Chapters of the National

All: Jim Wrinn

Volunteers are one of the keys to Spencer Shops revitalization. Just some of the many are depicted here:
From Left: As the N.C. Transportation Museum began planning a steam train ride, volunteers readied several coaches. Here volunteer Richard Morse of Charlotte fits a new window in a former Reading coach. Second from Left: Volunteer Doug Lyerly installs a new window sill in a coach. Center: Volunteer Archie Fisher paints the ceiling of a passenger coach in the winter of 1987. The museum's coaches were rebuilt before the passenger train began operating on Labor Day weekend that year. Upper right: Southern retiree Jim Mesimore at the throttle of engine No. 604. Lower right: Volunteer Donnie Smith nails siding on a Clinchfield caboose restored by the Samuel Spencer Chapter of the National Railway Historical Society.

David Driscoll/SRHA collection

Southern 2-8-0 locomotive No. 542, posed here in 1946, is the only Southern steam locomotive at the museum (after nearly 40 years at a Forsyth County park).

Railway Historical Society in Charlotte, Greensboro, Salisbury, and Roanoke, Va. gave significant contributions. The Hurley Foundation, created by Salisbury newspaper publisher Jim Hurley, gave $100,000. The Cannon Foundation in nearby Concord gave $75,000. The Kenan Foundation in Chapel Hill gave $50,000. The Duke Power Foundation gave $40,000. The Town of Spencer kicked in $20,000, and Rowan County came through with more than $100,000. The North Carolina General Assembly provided $250,000 in 1993 and $300,000 in 1994. In the end NCTHC, state government, individuals, corporations, and foundations pumped some $8 million into the project to revitalize the roundhouse and renew the museum.

Wagoner Construction Company of Salisbury won the general contract. Asbestos piping and lead paint were removed. A new roof was installed. New windows replaced broken panes. Concrete pillars and supports were repaired. New heating and cooling systems were installed. Tracks torn out of the roundhouse years earlier were replaced.

Plans for the roundhouse called for visitors to enter an orientation room in stalls three and four, then browse among restored rolling stock in stalls four through sixteen. They could peer into washrooms where workers once cleaned up and see inside the ticket office where employees received work orders. In one section would be 8,000 square feet of exhibits telling the story of Spencer Shops and railroading in North Carolina. In another area visitors would see volunteers at work on historic engines and cars in a heated, secure space after years outdoors in the elements.

Work on the roundhouse continued through 1994 and 1995. State officials awarded the project an extra $1.6 million. The museum enjoyed one of its best years ever in 1995 with 97,000 visitors. In the town of Spencer new businesses—three restaurants, a hobby shop, an art gallery, and other enterprises geared to tourists—sprang up. The town created one of the state's largest historic districts in the middle of downtown.

In January 1996 more than 100 museum supporters braved a blizzard to gather in the master mechanic's office for inaugural ceremonies marking the centennial of the shops. Outside snow fell several inches deep, but inside the museum was alive and warm with the knowledge that Samuel Spencer's namesake shops had finally blossomed in a second life, that thousands would learn the story of railroading at the museum. Steam railroading would not become a fading memory, the stuff of history books, but be preserved forever in this railroad town.

A committee of volunteers and staff members put together more than 100 events celebrating the Spencer Shops centennial. Capping the celebration was the planned grand opening of the roundhouse in September along with a new 300-car parking lot and completion of the Barber Junction Depot as the boarding area for the on-site train ride.

Another task force began identifying and restoring rail cars for exhibition in the roundhouse. More than 26 cars and locomotives were slated to go on display.

Much remains to be done at Spencer Shops, the museum. Plans to extend the rail ride to the Salisbury depot, a run of about three miles, were sidetracked by the high cost of insurance. And the mighty back shop, which saw attention in the museum's early years, got new doors in 1996 but little else. It awaits another new roof and windows to become the centerpiece of the museum. Plans call for it to become the main exhibit hall with emphasis on trucking and aviation.

In 1996 a stroll across the museum grounds yields both contrasts and similarities to the past. Where begrimed men once labored, families learn about the South's industrial heritage. In the newly renovated roundhouse, old engines and cars are still repaired. Across Salisbury Avenue, where shop workers once ate and did their business, tourists dine and browse and reflect on the giant industrial complex that once was and still is.

It is a fulfillment of a prophesy spoken back in the late 1950s when Southern Railway first laid off employees at Spencer. Someone asked if the the shops were to close, what would become of the town. Would it too fade away? In a true form of determination, the answer came: no—it would always be a railroad center. For once a railroad town, always a railroad town.

In spring 1988 the arduous task to reclaim tracks inside the roundhouse began. Here inmates from a nearby prison spread ballast. Tracks were installed in the last four bays of the building.

Before restoration, the roundhouse had changed little in the years since the railroad left. A hodge-podge of doors remained, and most of the windows were broken or in disrepair. This snow scene, in January 1988, shows a need for major work.

North Carolina Division of Archives and History
The former Buffalo Creek & Gauley 2-8-0 represents a Southern locomotive at Spencer Shops and provides the steam power for the on site train ride.